# GOD'S BUSINESS

# GOD'S BUSINESS

## HOW TO SUPERCHARGE
Your FAITH, Your PROFIT, and
Your CLIENT EXPERIENCE

FREDERICK "COACH" WEST III

New York

# GOD'S BUSINESS
HOW TO SUPERCHARGE Your FAITH, Your PROFIT, and Your CLIENT EXPERIENCE

Published in New York, New York, by Morgan James Publishing. Morgan James and The Entrepreneurial Publisher are trademarks of Morgan James, LLC.
www.MorganJamesPublishing.com

The Morgan James Speakers Group can bring authors to your live event. For more information or to book an event visit The Morgan James Speakers Group at www.TheMorganJamesSpeakersGroup.com.

## Shelfie
A **free** eBook edition is available
with the purchase of this print book.

CLEARLY PRINT YOUR NAME ABOVE IN UPPER CASE

**Instructions to claim your free eBook edition:**
1. Download the Shelfie app for Android or iOS
2. Write your name in **UPPER CASE** above
3. Use the Shelfie app to submit a photo
4. Download your eBook to any device

ISBN 978-1-63047-613-7 paperback
ISBN 978-1-63047-614-4 eBook
Library of Congress Control Number:
2015905203

**Cover Design by:**
Rachel Lopez
www.r2cdesign.com

**Interior Design by:**
Bonnie Bushman
bonnie@caboodlegraphics.com

In an effort to support local communities and raise awareness and funds, Morgan James Publishing donates a percentage of all book sales for the life of each book to Habitat for Humanity Peninsula and Greater Williamsburg

Get involved today, visit
www.MorganJamesBuilds.com

Habitat
for Humanity®
Peninsula and
Greater Williamsburg
Building Partner

# DEDICATION

This book is dedicated to my grandmother, Theresa Ayers, the woman who showed me that being a Christian is not a title, but rather who we are in our actions, inactions, and interactions everyday… Thank you for that gift, Grandma! <3

# TABLE OF CONTENTS

*Dedication*                                          *v*

*Preface*                                             *ix*

*Acknowledgments*                                     *xv*


**Section 1: A Life of Purpose Through Prosperity**    **1**

Chapter 1    Fulfilling Your Higher Purpose            3

Chapter 2    Customer Service is Killing Your Business  12

Chapter 3    The Separation of Church and Business Life 19


**Section 2: Transforming From Production to Purpose** **29**

Chapter 4    Time to Find the True Love In Your Life!   31

Chapter 5    Building Your Kingdom                      43

Chapter 6    Transforming Into a Provider              52

Chapter 7    The Power of Wisdom                        62

**Section 3: Shortening Your Walk Through the Desert**   **71**

Introduction    73

Chapter 8    Falling in Love With Your Product    75
is Killing Your Business

Chapter 9    Working the Jobsite is Killing Your Business    87

Chapter 10    Giving Out Raises is Killing Your Business    101

Chapter 11    The Call to Fulfilling Your Purpose    120
in the World

*Endnotes*    *125*

# PREFACE

When writing this book, there was such a conflict on where to start. On one hand, as a coach and consultant for over 15 years, I saw that on a fundamental level Christian businesses, like others, just didn't have access to the resources they needed to grow a thriving and scalable business. On the other hand, however, what I saw specifically holding Christian businesses back was the self-debilitating environment we had created for ourselves. In essence, I could delve right into how customer service is killing yours and so many other businesses, or I could "prepare the soil" and open up the beliefs that TRULY are holding Christian businesses back. So, after much prayer and discernment, I recalled one of my favorite parables, found in *Matthew 13: 39.* **Jesus told many stories such**

**as this one:** *"A farmer went out to plant some seed. As he scattered it across his field, some seeds fell on a footpath, and the birds came and ate them. Other seeds fell on shallow soil with underlying rock. The plants sprang up quickly, but they soon wilted beneath the hot sun and died because the roots had no nourishment in the shallow soil. Other seeds fell among thorns that shot up and choked out the tender blades. But some seeds fell on fertile soil and produced a crop that was thirty, sixty, and even a hundred times as much as had been planted. Anyone who is willing to hear should listen and understand!"*

It was then that I realized how foolish it would be to plant the seeds of knowledge onto ground that was not appropriately conditioned. As Christian business owners, it has become increasingly difficult to align our faith with our business. Something that was once a badge of honor we wore, symbolizing the values by which we ran our business, has now become a liability, and often a vehicle for judgment. When opening my own business, a coaching and consulting firm in 2009, I was nervous to associate my faith with my brand out of fear of not being "inclusive" enough. It was only recently that I decided —after a great amount of nudging from our Father in heaven that I had not been serving my brothers and sisters in Christ (or the world) to the best of my ability by keeping my faith quiet. It was tiring to witness Christian businesses getting attacked on all fronts. We were being attacked by people who do not share our beliefs. We were attacked and/or not supported by our government in more ways than I could count. Worst of all, we were attacking each other. You may be asking yourself, "How were we attacking each other?"

We must recognize that a profitable, thriving, Christian business is the greatest asset to our community, due to the values and charitable efforts that are a natural part of our faith. It was upsetting to me that often fellow Christians felt compelled to ask for discounts solely based on the fact that the business was owned by a Christian and we share the same faith.

Nowhere in our doctrine is this belief substantiated. In truth, the contrary is true…over and over again, we are called to be STEWARDS of his gifts he has given us (**Parable of the Talents** in **Matthew 25:14-30**) and to use them for his work!

After witnessing this for so many years in the business world, it plagued me enough to do something about it. Ultimately, it was the amount of satisfaction I gained in helping my fellow Christians, as well as the amount of success I was able to deliver to my Christian clients that finally compelled me to move in this direction. When discussing our need to provide for clients in business, and what our commitment means to our patrons, it just resonated more with people of faith. We noticeably "spoke" the same language, since the desire to provide for others came straight from the values of Christian life.

My grandmother always showed me that the best way to display our badge of faith was not necessarily to state it out loud, but to demonstrate it in every way possible, including how we communicate, how we deliver, and the care we show towards every relationship. It would be obvious even when meeting someone in the street by making such an impression on them that they felt compelled to ask, "Are you a Christian?"

Our faith has the opportunity to shine in all that we do, because the fundamentals of our faith give us the perfect blueprint on how to do it.

I wrote this book with the framework of a growing business that has several employees, that may have found itself stuck or looking for the next step. However, regardless of whether you are a multiple employee business, a one person operation, a non-profit, or a volunteer organization, the strategies laid out here still apply. In addition, while reading this book, you may find that you temporarily lack the necessary skills to fully take advantage of your new-found clarity. To that I would say the key to growing isn't having all the answers, but instead, knowing where to find them. Seek out people in your organization, or even outside of it, to fill in the gaps where you feel assistance is needed. This is not a time to be prideful, but rather a time to take appropriate action.

Finally, before you jump to any conclusions, allow me to clarify what this book is and what it isn't. This is not another religious book written about business, but rather, a business book that leverages our faith values to perform at a higher level. The intent is not necessarily to put more God into your business, but instead, give you a way to have more God shine through. It was written with the idea that we are Christians not by what we say, but by what we do; and through our actions people will just know that they are doing business with someone a little different. Now, I just wanted to alert you that I make MANY recommendations throughout the book for strategies and additional resources. However, I have also prepared a *God's Business Fast Action Guide* that highlights many of the keys and has direct links to everything you need to get started making the changes necessary to your business. The free download of this document can be found on www.GodsBusinessTheBook.com. So, sit back and prepare yourself for a new way to combine your faith and your business.

Download God's Business Fast Action Guide
www.godsbusinessthebook.com

# ACKNOWLEDGMENTS

I would like to thank first and foremost, my lovely wife, Clare West, mother of my eight (soon to be nine!) children, provider of my wonderful life, and my best friend, as well as my entire family for their support over the years as I discovered my calling and Higher Purpose in life! I would also like to thank my editor and fellow coach Rachelle Triay, without whom this book would not be where it is today.

I would also like to thank all the people who were sources of inspiration and values, including Pastor Ralph Fletcher, Father Jim Curran, Napoleon Hill, Bruce Wilkinson, Andy Andrews, John C. Maxwell, Ken Blanchard, Anthony Robbins, Dr. Joseph Murphy, Dr. W. Edwards Deming, Shane and Dannene Perry of Primerica Financial Services, and many others not mentioned here.

# Section 1

# A LIFE OF PURPOSE THROUGH PROSPERITY

## Chapter 1

# FULFILLING YOUR HIGHER PURPOSE

I am sure I am not the only one who is growing tired of hearing that we live in a new society, and that the times, and how we do business, are changing. Unfortunately, just because it has been said to exhaustion, doesn't mean it is any less true. The reach of our business and the reach of our clientele have evolved, and the way we were able to conduct business due to limited competition is no longer possible if we hope to maintain, or even grow. I am reminded of the story of the two boats and the helicopter. There are many versions, but they all go something like this:

*A terrible storm came into a town, and local officials sent out an emergency warning that the riverbanks would soon overflow and flood the nearby homes. They ordered everyone in the town to evacuate immediately. A faithful Christian man heard the warning and decided to stay, saying to himself, "I will trust God, and if I am in danger, then God will send a divine miracle to save me."*

*The neighbors came by his house and said to him, "We're leaving and there is room for you in our car, please come with us!" But the man declined. "I have faith that God will save me."*

*As the man stood on his porch watching the water rise up the steps, a man in a canoe paddled by and called to him, "Hurry and come into my canoe, the waters are rising quickly!" But the man again said, "No thanks, God will save me."*

*The floodwaters rose higher, pouring water into his living room and the man had to retreat to the second floor. A police motorboat came by and saw him at the window. "We will come up and rescue you!" they shouted. But the man refused, waving them off saying, "Use your time to save someone else! I have faith that God will save me!"*

*The flood waters rose higher and higher and the man had to climb up to his rooftop.*

*A helicopter spotted him and dropped a rope ladder. A rescue officer came down the ladder and pleaded with the man, "Grab my hand and I will pull you up!" But the man STILL refused, folding his arms tightly to his body. "No, thank you! God will save me!"*

*Shortly after, the house broke up and the floodwaters swept the man away.*

*He drowned.*

*When in Heaven, the man stood before God and asked, "I put all of my faith in You. Why didn't You come and save me?"*

*And God said, "Son, I sent you a warning. I sent you a car. I sent you a canoe. I sent you a motorboat. I sent you a helicopter. What more were you looking for?"*

For some of you, this book may be your car. For others, this may be your helicopter. What I am here to tell you is one thing: Customer Service as we knew it, and as it is interpreted today, is no longer sufficient.

From the root of its meaning to how people implement it today, it is flawed and as a result it is *killing* our businesses.

It was in early 2013 that I began to get the call to evolve my personal business. Frustrated about the negative associations our society has regarding Christian businesses, as well as the common problem of the misinterpretation of success and greed within our own faith community, I decided something needed to be done.

I began to share this with my friends and colleagues to see what they thought of evolving at least part of my practice to providing for the needs of Christian business owners specifically, and received mixed reviews. On one hand, there were a lot of warnings on what it meant to label yourself as a Christian business—including the idea that it meant you were not supposed to be profitable—and that it was more of a liability than an asset. On the other hand, I had one friend in particular, plainly say, "Fred, IT IS ABOUT TIME!"

She went on to say that we, as a Christian faith community, are under duress and need more "generals" on the battlefront.

The truth, as I have discovered, rang loud and clear on both sides.

It was in that moment that I knew that I was meant to fulfill my Higher Purpose by founding and building *Look Faith First*. It simply came down to the desperate need for something to empower Christian businesses back to living God's plan for them.

I did not come to this decision lightly, and now that I reflect on it, I may have been brought in kicking and screaming. For as long as I could remember, I held the belief that "God's work" could only be fulfilled in "God's place." I had the belief that even though I am a Christian and should act as one in everything I do, I was only able to fulfill God's Purpose for me when at church, on a retreat, or when participating in a ministry. It never occurred to me that the gifts and graces that were given to me professionally could —and SHOULD— be used for Him in every part of my life. While I could attempt to blame it on society's separation of church and state, in truth I knew deep down that it wasn't right and should have done something about it well before I did.

It was in this time of frustration and discernment that I turned to the Word, and was reminded of being "Stewards of

God's Grace" in *1 Peter: 4.* Written in the Scripture, right in front of me, was a mirror of my frustration: living with the gifts that God had bestowed on me, but fearful of what using those gifts could potentially expose my family and myself to. However, I could not ignore verses 10 through 11: *"As each one has received a gift, use it to serve one another as good stewards of God's varied grace. Whoever preaches, let it be with the words of God; whoever serves, let it be with the strength that God supplies, so that in all things God may be glorified through Jesus Christ, to whom belong glory and dominion forever and ever. Amen."*

The torture of my heart had been revealed, and there right in front of me was the answer. It was time for me to be the STEWARD of the gifts God bestowed on me… and my spiritual side knew it.

To prevent this oversight from ever happening again, I came up with three rules as the beacon of my life.

First, I committed to make myself **available** to whatever God's Purpose was for me. I eliminated my "rules" around when it was appropriate, where it was appropriate, and/or what is or is not "socially" acceptable.

Second, I committed to make myself **able** to fulfill God's Purpose for me. I constantly explore opportunities to learn from failure or success, and I committed to increase my education and acumen every day.

Third, I committed to make myself **aware** to fulfill God's Purpose for me. I look at every situation in my life as purposeful, and with the idea that God has a reason for it. I specifically looked for opportunities He uses to direct me, to grow me, or to put me in a place to have an impact.

It was when I fully embraced these concepts that I knocked down the walls that were holding me back from answering my calling, and that is why I am now in front of you. After making the decision to embrace my new calling of helping Christian businesses and organizations, I immediately went to action. If you are reading this book, it is for a reason. Most likely it is because of one or two things: Either you are holding yourself back, OR you know someone being called to fulfill their Purpose that isn't. With this clear vision and fresh resolve, I knew the best place to start would be to eliminate the things holding the majority of Christian businesses and organizations back from fulfilling their Higher Purpose right now: their beliefs.

More specifically, we as Christian business owners hold back because of the beliefs we have about **ourselves**, or the beliefs we have about what it **means** to be a Christian business.

When it comes to beliefs we have about ourselves, many of us start out in very humble beginnings and go on to be successful, far exceeding what we or anyone else expected from us. This often makes the idea of expanding even more frightening, if you believe you ALONE are the one who has to do it. However, were you truly ever doing it alone? All of us have had those moments in our lives where we just knew that God, our partner, was with us, and that our partner was guiding and protecting us along the way. Maybe even in the pages of this book, you are getting the answers on how you can grow even more, and the way you came across it was complete "coincidence." We have the best partner in the world, my friend... one who has our interests and the interests of the greater good first on His heart. He is great and powerful, and wants you to succeed. Not only that, but He knows the path, and wants you to walk it. If you can just recognize and constantly remind yourself of this one thing, imagine the difference it would make!

The other misguided belief has to do with what it means to be a Christian business owner. The belief that Christian businesses are not supposed to be profitable, and that focusing on money, in itself, is a sin, is not only *devastating* for the financial stability of your business, but also for the ministries and charities you are called to support. In short, it can be what is truly holding you back from fulfilling the Purpose God has had for you all along.

For example, one of the most misinterpreted Scriptures is **1 Timothy 6:10**, that "Money is the root of all evil" Let me first clarify that the Scripture actually reads that it is the **"love of money that is the root of all evil,"** not the money itself. Another example is the **Parable of the Rich Man and Lazarus** in **Luke 16:1931**. The "rich man" in the parable was not the villain of the story because of the money he made, but rather what he did (or didn't) do with it. I WILL SAY IT AGAIN: YOU ARE ALLOWED TO BE PROFITABLE as a business. As long as you are providing what you are promising, running your business with integrity, and delivering to your clients the experience you promised, being profitable is allowed. In addition to the blessings God can bestow on others through you, it allows us to be the shining example of what it *really* means to be a "Christian Business": operating with Christian values at heart…and with the profits justly earned.

To clarify, here is a summary of the most detrimental beliefs Christian Businesses hold on to:

**The "Scarcity Belief"** "If someone else has something, that means I have-not, and in order to have more, I must take from those who have, or be miserly with what I already possess." The truth is, we serve a God of abundance. Nowhere does He say that if we "have," others are without as a result. Instead, we are called to share our wealth and success for the benefit of all around us, and the only way to do so is to accumulate it first.

**The "Wealth Belief"** As previously mentioned, nowhere does the bible say Christians are not supposed to accumulate wealth. The idea we are not supposed to be prosperous because of money being the root of all evil and the rich man's path to heaven being tighter that a hole in a needle is a farce. The truth is it is not the accumulation of wealth, but rather how we use it, that we should be conscious of. Money is like any other tool available to us today, like the internet, automobiles or even words. It is not the object's properties that are good or evil, but how it is utilized.

**The "Profitability Belief"** The belief is that Christian Businesses are not supposed to be profitable. It saddens me that many feel compelled to ask for discounts and considerations from our fellow Christians, when instead we should be supporting their prosperity, knowing that our faith calls them to do FANTASTIC things with the wealth and gifts they have accumulated.

The proliferation of these beliefs throughout the Christian community has truly been the biggest obstacle holding us back from fulfilling God's Purpose for us all.

Another great fear I have seen among Christian business owners is the concern about what type of person you will become if success were to find you. I have read the same stories, and seen the same tragedies that have come from the accumulation of great wealth. To be honest, it is true that money only amplifies who we are, and that there is risk in becoming wealthy. All I can say is: That is why it is so important to realize and remember NOW that God is your business partner, and recognize that He is entitled to His share of your business success. Find a coach or a spiritual guide you trust that will help you to keep your partner close, and make sure that OUR LORD is part of every decision.

Summed up briefly, CHRIST NEEDS US to fulfill our Higher Purpose, so that we are able to do His work with the time we have here in this world. Do not fear success, but instead, welcome it, and use it for the good that God needs done.

## Chapter 2

# CUSTOMER SERVICE IS KILLING YOUR BUSINESS

W hen reflecting on the Christian business community, one of the most troubling things to witness is the natural barriers they put between their faith and their business life. If you were to ask most Christian businesses what their greatest strength is, the first thing that comes up 99% of the time is Customer Service... But, truly, that would be the same for any other business as well. As a result, the idea of Customer Service has become undifferentiating. It provides very little separation from competition, or even other product or service offerings that are available to people every day.

With all the noise that we are inundated with on a daily basis, Customer Service alone rings as loud as one car on a major highway. In addition, how business owners and their employees interpret Customer Service can range anywhere from "I was nice to them wasn't I?" to "I gave them what they wanted." The truth is we implement Customer Service based on what we, personally, interpret it to be in our own lives. This is one profound reason there can be such a huge divide in its interpretation. If you didn't know already, being "nice" or "considerate" of our customer is a minimum, and really nothing to strive for.

Another fundamental flaw with the fascination with Customer Service is how we measure it according to customer satisfaction. There was a great book written by Ken Blanchard back in 1993, called *Raving Fans,1* that delves into this topic much deeper, and I highly suggest that you put it on your MUST READ list. In short, the book does a great job of opening up the limitations we have on Customer Service, and cautions against measuring your effectiveness on customer satisfaction surveys, because satisfying our customers is *too easy*. The reason is that the expectation is for us, as businesses, to mess up somehow anyway, and as long as we are minimally competent in the delivery of our product, they are "satisfied." Talk about uninspiring… but it is hard to deny the truth in that statement. We have all had that one Customer Service experience so awful, that anything that DIDN'T end in a similar way just might get a decent review on such a survey. Unfortunately, with a standard so low, "satisfaction" as a measurement becomes grossly inaccurate compared to what your customers might really need.

The problem lies, fundamentally, with the term itself. When looking closer at the meanings behind the words in the phrase "Customer Service," there is already a clear conflict of intent based on the root definition. Many years ago, a manager of mine changed my entire interpretation of the difference between a "Customer" and a "Client." I was struggling in a new industry as a consultant, and in a moment of frustration I began to vent during a new sales representative training class. I can't really recall how I started the conversation or what I even said, however, I will gladly share what has stuck with me from that day on.

Manager: "Fred, why are you going out every day and looking for customers?"

Me: "Well, I don't have anyone to do business with, what else am I *supposed* to do?"

Manager: "So, is that what you are looking for... Someone to simply do business with?"

(I was reaching the point of irritation and confusion at this point...)

Me: *"Isn't that why we are here?"*

Manager: "Well, I tell you what... I, personally, have never had luck with finding Customers in this business either. However, I find that I do an excellent job with developing relationships with my Clients."

Still a little frustrated, but at the same time intrigued, I asked him to expand on the difference. He went on to describe to me that there are businesses where a relationship as a "Customer" is acceptable. If you are working in the fast food drive through or at the ticket counter at the theatre, transacting business with a "Customer" is fine. Your prospect has decided on what they want, has no need for your expertise, and already has their money in hand. For them, at the moment, the only thing standing in the way of getting what they want is you taking their money and giving a receipt. HOWEVER, in any type of relationship that requires expertise, the demands are much higher.

What I gathered from him, if my primary focus was just on getting a listing or showing a house, the people I was working with would be able to sense that. On the other hand, if my commitment was to protect one of their biggest assets, or ensure they get the best home that their hard earned dollars could purchase, I would be the "partner" they were looking for and honestly… *deserved*. The differentiation between a "Customer" and a "Client" was a defining moment for me. From that moment on, I made a commitment to refine myself personally and my craft professionally through everything I did. I never wanted to work the drive-through; therefore, I would never look for a "Customer" again.

Over the years, I have observed other distinctions that separate the engagement some representatives have compared with others when dealing with qualified prospects. The two most pronounced observations that stand out to me are "The Type of Relationship" and the "Level of Care". The type of relationship, whether a "Customer" or a "Client," was very clear to me… I either focused on the transaction or the mutual partnership. However, it was after observing businesses and sales representatives for over a decade that I saw there was still something missing in distinguishing one representative over another. On one hand, I could see many representatives dedicate the same time, professionalism, and expertise in the relationship with their prospects. However, there were certain ones that were just a little different. Then it hit me… these select individuals truly had *compassion* for the people which they were "Providing" for.

The majority of people who interact with others do so because they are paid to do so. Interestingly enough, "Service" is actually derived from the Latin word *"servitium"* which means "condition of a slave." Now, let's be honest… very few people know the true definition consciously. That being said, I have also had many conversations with employers and employees that have compared dealing with a customer to being "slavery." At the very least, many people interpret "service" to mean meeting the needs of people out of *obligation*, and how fulfilling is that, really? Some people have gone so far as to having a feeling of inferiority while "serving" others, and as a result have to deal with a huge internal conflict while performing their required duties.

So, in putting these two words together for a literal interpretation of the phrase, good "Customer Service" is your hope to "transact business out of obligation." As the phrase implies, your only commitment is that you will deliver to those who inquire with *only* what they specifically request, and *only* while they are there… treating every transaction as an isolated, permanent event. Is that what you meant when committing to "Customer Service"?

I highly doubt it…

But how often do you get the feeling that your team and/or company feel that way while working with prospects? It is long overdue to reinvent how we do business and the standards by which we operate, don't you think? We have had the answer all along my brothers and sisters, and it is time to put it into action. It is time to start PREACHING where we PRACTICE.

*What you absolutely need to know from chapter 2:*

1. Customer Service as we knew it, and as it is interpreted today, is no longer sufficient.
2. If you didn't know already, being "nice" or "considerate" of our customers is a minimum, and really nothing to strive for.
3. It is time to reinvent how we do business, and the standards by which we operate.

*Chapter 3*

# THE SEPARATION OF CHURCH AND BUSINESS LIFE

few years back, I was approached by a business owner while attending an after-hours event with the local Christian Chamber. After taking turns around the room introducing our businesses, a man came over with haste after hearing I was a business coach and consultant. My first inclination was that he wanted to find out more about what I did, but in reality, "Bob" wanted to find a kindred spirit to support his views on how complicated business was. He proceeded to describe all the decisions, actions, and nuances a business owner had to endure, and was almost offended that it would take someone like me to help make it livable. While he was talking, a small crowd started to gather around our conversation, and some of them were murmuring in agreement. After he finished his mind-dump in the middle of the room, he awaited my response.

"Bob," I asked, "When you describe all of these decisions, you make it sound as if they are all isolated from one another." He nodded as if to say, "Of course I did."

So I continued, "Ok... so, Bob, who drives all these decisions? Meaning, what acts as the catalyst to provoke them, and what do you base the decision off of?"

He replied, "Well, I am the owner, so I base it off of what I feel is right," with even more annoyance.

"Well, there is the first issue, Bob...When was the last time you asked the *clients you provide for* what they wanted or need from you?"

His face changed, and he began to think about it. It didn't take long after, with a few more questions, for Bob to realize that every decision was interlinked. That the pressure he put on himself to make the best decision on his own—with no input from those he provided for—was in itself a daunting task...A task which could be much easier, and possibly even enjoyable, if he had communicated with the people who were actually benefiting from his product.

What Bob was feeling is common, and quite honestly, it's not Bob's fault he was doing it wrong!

Frankly, this is a typical scenario for a business owner. They get so used to making the decisions for their business, that it becomes natural to internalize the decisions for how to "serve" their client. Serving, though, is about taking orders and delivering on them with very little thought or prejudice. The relationship we have with our clients, however, should be looked at in a different light. The connection with our clients should compare more with the role we have with others under our care, like children or adults who are not able to provide for themselves. We do not serve them… what we do instead is provide for their needs by anticipating and by taking responsibility. They continue under our care until someone else has taken responsibility. So in the grander scheme of things, it wasn't Bob's fault that he viewed his role this way. When all you are doing is focusing on "Customer Service" and trying to deliver out of obligation the wants— not needs—of those who call on us, it can become very overwhelming, unsatisfying, and stressful.

When anyone asks me about the secret of running a successful business, I always tell them that all they have to do is take what they learn on Sunday, and use it every day of the week. As Christians, we are called to "provide for those in need," and as a business owner, it is *no different*. When most people volunteer for a ministry, especially when they are taking care of others in need, they have a great amount of peace and enjoyment. It certainly isn't because of the pay, or because it is easy work, or even because everyone you come in contact with is pleasant. In reality, it is because through your hands someone's needs were met, and there is a satisfaction in doing that worth more than money.

So why are patrons of your business any different?

In the previous chapter, we discussed the ineffectiveness of "Customer Service." It was delivery of a product or service out of obligation with no intent of a long term relationship. We may say "Come back" in our words, but are there consistent, active efforts to provide for them after they leave our place of business or after the contract is satisfied? Do your employees interact with them as if they will be seeing them again, or do you find that you, as the owner, are driving the entire relationship on your own? It is in this way, and many others I have mentioned before, that "Customer Service," as a commitment, falls short of our true intent. It is the very reason we get no satisfaction from what we do every day… and our clients can feel it!

What we should instead focus on is "Client Provision."

The definition of "Client" is derived from the Latin *client-, cliens*; perhaps akin to Latin *clinare*, meaning "to lean." "Provide" comes from the Latin *providēre*, literally "to see ahead", from *pro-* (forward) + *vidēre* (to see). So, if we accepted our role as "One who looks ahead for someone who is leaning on us," how would that change the way you and your team look and interact with your clients? In addition, when we "provide" for others, it isn't done out of obligation, but instead out of PASSION… which is why we gain so much joy out of it in the first place. With an intention like this at the forefront of our vision, what type of difference would it make for your patrons, the growth of your business, and the satisfaction your team gets from what they do?

In *looking ahead for those who lean on us*, is it too ambitious to expect us to prepare our business to meet the needs of our clients, deliver on those needs at the level promised, and then maintain the connection even after the current transaction is done? If it isn't, then THIS is what can set you apart in the business world.

One final thing I would like to clarify is that to "provide" for our clients' needs does not mean to "provide" for ALL of their needs. A big part of the commitment to care for others that lean on us is for us to recognize that we *may not* be the people best suited or equipped to do so. We have to be honest about our capabilities with others, and most especially, with ourselves. Trying to be everything to everyone just means you are specifically committed to no one. Examine your business, and take a true inventory with what you can, can't, and are willing or unwilling to do. Then commit to what you can consistently provide for those who call on you to do so. "Client Provision" isn't something that you say you do; it is the agreement that you are committing to with every transaction.

However, it isn't enough to say that we are committing to "Client Provision"... it is the actions we take *after* the commitment that proves it or not.

*What you need to know from chapter 3:*

1. Business decisions can be far less stressful, or even enjoyable, if you communicate with those who benefit from your product.
2. Treating work with your clients like you would a ministry of providing to those in need helps focus on your calling as a business owner: to provide.
3. Looking ahead and anticipating your client's needs will set you apart in the business world, but it is not enough to simply commit. You MUST act.

# End of Section 1

Congratulations on completing the foundational pieces of creating and cultivating God's Business! As previously mentioned, when initially writing this book, I was naturally inclined to delve right into the specific strategies and tools to enhance and immediately grow a business. However, through some reflection and prayer I realized that most business owners ALREADY KNOW the many of the immediate enhancements and changes they can make to have a more prosperous, purposeful, and impactful business. So, why is it that most Christian businesses fall so short on their Purpose? It is because the faith in the Purpose of their business and themselves has been built on a foundation of sand.

**Mathew 7:24-27** says:

**24 "Therefore everyone who hears these words of mine and puts them into practice is like a wise man who built his house on the rock. 25 The rain came down, the streams rose, and the winds blew and beat against that house; yet it did not fall, because it had its foundation on the rock. 26 But everyone who hears these words of mine and does not put them into practice is like a foolish man who built his house on sand. 27 The rain came down, the streams rose, and the winds blew and beat against that house, and it fell with a great crash.**

What is so elegantly portrayed here is that power does not come from *knowledge* alone. Rather, the power comes from the *application of knowledge*. It is not enough to say that you are a believer. It is about having the lifestyle and the conviction that represents it. It is not enough to say that you are a steward of His gifts. It is about having your *actions and decisions represent* that you are a steward of His gifts. It is not enough to say that your business is "God's Business" if you are not willing to represent that in *every* interaction, transaction, and choice.

Are you wondering what this means for you?

Are you unsure as to how you can apply your knowledge in order to advance your business and realize your Higher Purpose?

If so, we have created *God's Business Fast Action Guide* to accompany this book. This guide will help you put your knowledge into a clear plan that brings meaningful results. You can download your guide at www. GodsBusinessTheBook.com.

Between this book and your God's *Business Fast Action Guide*, the only thing that will hold you back from having the business you were anointed to have is **you**. Enjoy the rest of the book, make sure to take action going forward, and receive the blessing that comes from fulfilling the Purpose God has for you!

Download God's Business Fast Action Guide
www.godsbusinessthebook.com

Section 2

# TRANSFORMING FROM PRODUCTION TO PURPOSE

## Chapter 4

# TIME TO FIND THE
# TRUE LOVE IN YOUR LIFE!

One of the hardest transitions from a "Customer Service" mindset to that of a "Client Provision" mindset is the adoption of how the owner views their business. Since most owners start out not in the college classroom, but instead on the jobsite, it is easy for them to believe they are in the business of their trade and not in the business of providing for the needs of their clients. For example, when the automobile industry started growing in the United States, many businesses were horrified... especially the horse and buggy dealers. As the cost of owning an automobile began to drop and the capabilities and reliability of the automobiles increased, they saw the need for their product (which was a long and lasting tradition in the consumer and commercial industry) rapidly evaporate. Imagine if more of those companies that manufactured, supplied, and maintained the horse and buggy had adapted their business like Studebaker did, and evolved with the times. Do you believe that they would have suffered the same fate?

By 1868, the five Studebaker brothers had become quite successful businessmen. Henry and Clem had made a reputation building wagons in South Bend, Indiana during the Gold Rush, and John M. built them in California for the Army. With the proceeds, John M. put into production the first Studebaker horse and buggy, which became wildly popular. Their brother, Peter, ran a General store in Goshen, Indiana, and in seeing a great opportunity, expanded his operation to include wagons and buggies, which the Army ordered from him during the Civil War. After the great success they had in dealing with each other, the brothers decided to merge and form Studebaker Brothers Manufacturing. In less than 10 years, they had the largest vehicle house in the world. Their products were so much in demand that in 1889, incoming President Harrison ordered a whole line of Studebaker carriages and harnesses for the White House.[2]

By 1895, though, with the paving of roads and the introduction of the motor vehicle, Peter Studebaker's son-in-law Fred Fish realized they were going to have to make a change if the company was going to survive. Piggybacking on the original five brother's vision for expansion, he realized they were not in the "horse and buggy" business, but rather, in the "transportation" business. After a lot of experimentation, and an eventual partnership, Studebaker produced its first line of gasoline powered "horseless carriages" in 1904. Over the next 50 years, Studebaker held the standard in quality and prestige, and became one of the better success stories of their time.

The lesson here is to never fall in love with your product… instead, fall in love with your *client*. This understanding and foresight must be adapted from the top-down. Business owners that attach how they define their business too closely with a specific product or service risk becoming obsolete when that product or service nears the end of its life. This is one of the major reasons it is so dangerous for the owner to spend the majority of his time with a hammer in his or her hand, managing projects at the site, or working the counter. As he or she plays out the role of a provider of services, he or she never really has the time to focus on the future of his or her business or industry. In truth, the owner's role in his or her business should be to:

1. Develop, maintain, evolve, and share the vision of his or her business to the team
2. Instill belief in his or her team that the vision can be obtained, and that they are capable as a company of obtaining it

3. Provide the environment and motivation by which the business can meets its vision

4. Deliver the tools and training needed in its obtainment

5. Supply the plan and system by which they will obtain it

As a business owner or a manager, how much of your time is spent in the aforementioned capacities in comparison to putting out fires, managing projects, or dealing directly with the public?

After working with businesses for over a decade, I know first-hand the reasons why they don't fulfill their roles. Some of these are lack of trust in those around them, fear of tarnishing their good name, and getting caught up in the story that "this is the life a business owner signs up for." But really, all these mentalities have done is bottleneck your business and taken the power and potential away from your team. As a result, there is very little chance that you can fully provide for the needs of your clients, and chances are you will do very little towards providing for them at a higher level in the future. By fulfilling the above five goals, you can transform your business from a top-down accountability model to one with a culture of accountability. Rather than you being the driver of enforcement and standards, your business as its own entity will do that for you and, in addition, hold you accountable for fulfilling your role for it. As mentioned before, too many business owners align how they define themselves directly with their business, which provokes them to try and control every aspect of it. I often relay to my clients that the government and their clients view their business as a living, breathing, tax-paying entity... so why don't you?

In much the same way, it isn't we who are providing for the poor or others in need, it is our Lord and Savior working through us. I realize what a mental shift this is for many business owners and/or managers, and I also realize how tall of an order this is to fill. However, please don't get overwhelmed! I wouldn't make such a case if I didn't plan on sharing more with you on HOW to do it.

The image a business projects is created from the first exposure with the client, and confirmed through every subsequent interaction. This could be from the product or service provided, your marketing efforts, an employee out in the general public, or even a past client sharing their positive or negative experience. This is why it is so VERY important that we are DELIBERATE and INTENTIONAL about the image we project. It is amazing to realize that at *any* time you may be gaining or losing opportunities not based on facts, but merely on the *interpretation* a potential client has about what they experience.

For companies and organizations that have been clear and deliberate on what they project to the world, this understanding comes with a great amount of pride and confidence. However, for most it could be a scary idea to digest, understanding the scope of every action and interaction. It is up to you as the owner to discern who you want to be for those you provide for, and ensure that *every* aspect of your business is congruent in projecting that image.

We can more simply illustrate the whole thing below:

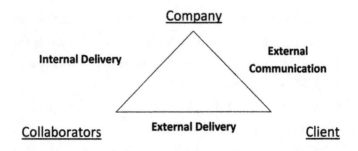

What we have above is a variation of Philip Kotler and Waldemar Pfoertsch's "Branding Triangle" from their book, *B2B Brand Management*. Each side of the triangle represents the parties involved in the operation of a business. At the very top we see the "General Public," which is an outside view and interpretation of how the business is represented. At the top point of the triangle, you have the living, breathing entity represented to the world: the "Company." At the bottom left corner, we have the "Collaborators," which are the people that represent the company. Finally, on the bottom right corner, we have the "Client," who directly interacts with both parts of the business representation. Generally, this diagram is used in designing marketing campaigns; however, it also does a great job representing the responsibilities each entity has towards the client. In between the Company and Client we have a two-way communication. The Company is constantly communicating with the Client on how they are equipped and committed to fill their needs. The company is also constantly assessing and determining through direct or indirect contact whether they are providing for the needs of their client, and how they can meet the needs at a higher level. Between the Collaborators and the Client we have the delivery on the promises made by the Company, and also the communication from the Client on how their needs need to be specifically addressed. Finally, between the Company and the Collaborators we have the internal delivery of the Company. The Company is continually relaying what they are promising, supplying the tools by which to deliver it, and keeping a fixed view on how they may have to provide for the needs of the Client in the future. In addition, the Collaborators are relaying how effectively they are fulfilling the need of the Client, as well as ideas on how to improve delivery. In this chapter, we covered the role of the Company in this equation. Later on we will focus on the role the Collaborators play.

One of the biggest challenges for businesses whose owners have built their company from the ground up is that the priorities in the beginning were about producing an income and not what they intend to represent. Some businesses can go on for years—or even decades—without investing any time or effort into discovering their true purpose or intention. It doesn't really become a problem until the owner, out of necessity, must begin delegating to his team, and he or she is no longer there to represent the company and uphold the standard. This goes far beyond developing a "Vision Statement," a "Mission Statement," a "Motto," etc. It is about being very intentional on who your company is, what your company will deliver to those who call on you, and how your company will deliver it.

I realize that many people probably feel like they have done this before. They have communicated and shared THEIR standards with others before and no one implemented them consistently, but therein lies the problem. They were YOUR standards and not the standards the company projected and shared itself.

Inconsistencies in standards as an organization can be DEVASTATING for quality. If there is a difference of standards between you and parts of your leadership group, if there a difference between whether there is "time" on the job to fulfill those standards, or even if it is contingent on the mood and/or focus of the ownership, any inconsistency can be detrimental. The only way to have consistent standards is to have them created and communicated at the company level.

Once the company has a clear definition about who it is and to whom a consistent image can be projected, then the company can direct the Values, Beliefs, and Attitudes of those representing it to be congruent with the new image. Then and ONLY THEN will the people representing the company intentionally raise their OWN standards and gain the hyper-awareness to notice when those standards are or are not being met.

The systems that I regularly share with my personal business clients to facilitate this transition works in three phases:

1. A business must **DECLARE** what they represent
2. Then **DEFINE** what that means
3. Finally, **DETERMINE** the standards and actions by which they will fulfill the Vision.

During the DECLARE stage of vision development a business must discern who it is that they will provide for and what they want to represent to their client. The advantages of having these two questions answered are well documented. Some of the more notable ones are a clearer message, easier conflict resolution, and a definite beacon to keep a business on their desired path. The recommendation I give to businesses that may be still searching for those answers, or that are looking to answer it more deliberately is a tool called the "Value Proposition Canvas."[3]

When moving into the DEFINE stage, the business gains clarity on how exactly they will set up their business to deliver on that vision, what will they provide, where will they provide it, how will they provide it, etc. Quite often established businesses already have answered many of these questions. However, if they were answered out of necessity rather than intention (which they often are) then it is a "best practice" to review this phase with an open mind. A great tool I suggest for new and established businesses to use is the "Business Model Canvas."[4]

Finally, in the DETERMINE stage, the business has the opportunity to be intentional with the standard by which they provide for the client and what type of experience they want to deliver. Being very definite on the standards of delivery and the actions by which to deliver those standards creates a world-class operation in every phase, and a world-class experience for your clients, which is the epitome of "Client Provision." While there are many organizations that have figured out their own ways of doing so, few, if any, have mastered it at the level Ritz Carlton has with their "Gold Standard." Rather than explain at length how and what they do, there have been COUNTLESS books and articles written on the topic. One of my favorites to date is *The New Gold Standard* by Joseph Michelli.[5] They are VERY deliberate in every decision, action, and result when interacting with the client (Not to mention, their parent company, Marriott, is owned by a Christian family). So I would suggest every business owner make an effort to discover more about what the Ritz Carlton is doing, and how.

To summarize this chapter in a few words from the Good Book, ***Proverbs 29:18*** starts out with ***"Where there is no vision the people will perish."*** Though biblically, this meant for man to keep a focus on God's laws, it rings true in every part of life… even in business. Without a vision, a business will perish… and unless that vision is based on true intent, they will never be able to stay true to their core Purpose.

Finally, sharing that vision and how to obtain it with those who will be delivering it will ensure that the business keeps its focus where it should be.

*What you need to know from chapter 4:*

1. Business owners that attach how they define their business too closely with a specific product or service risk becoming obsolete when that product or service nears the end of its life.

2. By delivering to your customers the "Client Provision" they deserve, you can transform your business from a top-down accountability model to that of a culture of accountability.

3. Without a Vision, a business will perish... and unless that Vision is based on the owner's true intent, it will never be able to stay true to its core Purpose.

## Chapter 5

# BUILDING YOUR KINGDOM

A word of caution for the remainder of this book: Just as I have preached about having a specific vision and a specific intent in how you are doing business, I have a specific intent for the order of these chapters.

A lot of what I have written here is part of a common conversation I have with my clients. We start with realizing the right intent, building the vision, and so on... until we reach the point on how to put everything into action. What I have learned over the last decade of consulting is like anyone else, business owners are creatures of habit. The most common impulse is to take immediate action, so that they justify the investment of time and money.

They will go to their teams, tell them everything that they are changing (with no specifics, I might add) and create a huge amount of anxiety inside their business.

I am telling you now, HOLD THE URGE!!!

Take the time to fully realize your vision and your intent with "providing for your client."

Take a moment. Figure out how you can deliver on that vision, and what changes can—and will—be made. Have a plan based on that intent, and prioritize the changes based on what is going to give you the biggest leap towards your intention, with the least amount of investment of time, resources, and adverse impact.

Stated briefly, start with the first four chapters of this book, and do everything you can on your own… so that once you share your vision with your team, it is inspiring instead of confusing. The more realistic the vision is when presented, the less likely they are to reject it or dismiss it as the "new flavor of the month." It is more likely they will embrace it, and even aid in its implementation and development.

SO, AGAIN…HOLD BACK!!

Got it?

Great.

Ok, back to business.

So…assuming now that we have a vision and the right intent for a business, we can begin the process of getting our "Collaborators" involved. In a business where the vision is fully realized and fully embraced by everyone involved, amazing things can happen. The owner no longer drives the standards from the top-down, but instead, the core vision of the business drives everyone. As a result, other managers and facilitators are able to redirect their time to improvement and innovation, and spend less time implementing minimal standards for the people under their care.

Does this sound like a dream come true? Well, it can come true if your business is set up for that dream to germinate and flourish. One of the most common complaints I get from business owners is that many of their subordinates just show up at work for a paycheck. They have little or no loyalty to the ones they are serving, to the job they do, or to the business that employs them. My immediate response to that is, "Well…what do you provide for your people other than financial compensation?" Often, I get a dumbfounded look as if to say, "What else can I give them?" On occasion, I get a laundry list of benefits including healthcare, retirement benefits, education grants, and so on. But all of it amounts to strategic ways to give monetary compensation which means…YES, THEY ARE THERE TO GET A PAYCHECK.

Sometimes, you may be blessed with a person who has the work ethic and dedication to look beyond that. You can attempt to follow the policy of hiring slow and firing fast and build a team based on, in essence, smart gambling. The Christian alternative, however, is to have an environment that provides more than just compensation…

one that attracts the people you are seeking. My favorite example of this is the well-known Christian business, Chik-Fil-A. I cannot remember a time when I was treated rudely, or if there was a mistake, it wasn't immediately resolved with some sort of offering of restitution. There were times where the mistake, in my eyes, was trivial at most... but they treated it with the utmost importance and worked quickly to remedy it. I love that they stay true to their Christian values and are closed on Sundays (which is harder to accept when I am craving the sandwich!), and that they are not ashamed of their faith. So, do you believe that they are just luckier than other fast food providers on the same street? Do you believe that their interview process is so awesome that they can find the perfect person to work for under $15 dollars an hour in any store through the country?

OF COURSE, NOT.

They have an environment that not only attracts, but also provides for people who work inside of it. I know of many young people who would take less money an hour just to be a part of that company. So what is their secret, and the secret of others like them? They have what I call a L.O.V.E.-ing environment.

**L** oyalty

**O** wnership

**V** ibrance

**E** xemplify

We will delve into this topic much deeper later in the book, but here is a quick summary of each.

**Loyalty**- When most business owners speak of loyalty, generally, the focus is placed on the loyalty of the employee to the company, and not necessarily the loyalty the company shows to the team.

Can we be realistic?

Unless you are an emerging company in an emerging market, entry level people will outgrow your opportunity at some point and move on. Is this because they are not loyal? Of course not! This is because having a person that isn't evolving or growing is a travesty. Whether that growth is within your organization or they move on somewhere else, the growth of people is a great thing. How committed are you to their success, regardless where they have it?

Immediate steps you can take to increase loyalty in your business:

1. Understand that loyalty is a two-way street.
2. Set the standard in your first interaction. Be committed to their success regardless of if it is with you or not and let them know you expect them to be committed to the success of your company, also.
3. Like everything else, great people are developed! Always be training them, making them better.
4. Compassion extends beyond work. Support them whenever you can, and try to give them skills that will translate to all parts of their lives.

**Ownership**- Do you allow employees to take ownership of their role in your company?

Employees who constantly focus on improving have higher potential and produce at a higher level. It also is an example of your commitment to their ongoing success. Whether you bring in training professionals, have in an house training coordinator, or designate outside courses there are always ways to improve. The more you are focused on delivering the tools necessary for ownership, the more focused they will be on taking ownership in everything they are doing.

**Vibrance**- ENTHUSIASM IS CONTAGIOUS. If people have an environment like a Christian Retreat to go to everyday, how much would they dread the trip? There is just something to be said about ENERGY! When you have it, things move fast, and tempo goes up...It's almost like a well-oiled track with no friction at all moving from one stage to the next. Without it... well anyone who has been in a negative environment knows what it is like. It is a constant battle to get anyone to do anything, even if it is simple and in their job description. "Community Commitment" is almost non-existent, and "watching out for number one" is common place. People want to be inspired, they want to be swooned, and they want to be LIT UP!!! They want to lose the hours, and not even realize where they have all gone. Our fear of judgment here in the United States has caused us to become complacent, content, and bored... always searching for something that will distract us (Facebook, anyone?). Find ways to get your team excited, and make that the standard of your business. Don't let "being cool" get in the way of your team's enjoyment, and promote some type of competition everywhere you can. I'm not talking about sales contests and overwhelming standards, I am talking about things that are fun and that promote working together and critical thinking… Make it fun! I mean come on, HIGH FIVES ARE FREE. There will be more tools and examples on this ahead in the chapter "Giving Out Raises is Killing Your Business".

**Exemplify**- Exemplify the people who take action towards your vision. Far too often, we only recognize those who are not doing the right thing or that are increasing sales. If you look at that action objectively, what you are saying is that as long as your employees don't do anything wrong, and make sales for the company they are your kind of guy or gal… If that was the true case, I doubt you would have made it reading this far.

As you are making changes in your business, recognize the people who are taking ownership of them. If there is a guy or gal who constantly makes suggestions and is really participating, make an example of them. Be careful, though… people will only do what gets recognized and monitored, so be clear in your expectations of people, and be your own example of what you are encouraging in your environment.

Great managers are made, not born, and the same can be said about great employees, to a degree. You will be amazed at the opportunities that are uncovered by creating a L.O.V.E.ing environment, and those you are called on to provide for will reap the benefits, too. I am sure you are familiar with "Hate begets hate, and love begets love." Well, the same can be true how we show love to those who aid in accomplishing our vision... Our vision begets other's vision. Inspire others with your vision, and I am sure you will see a whole other level of commitment from those that work for you.

***What you need to know from chapter 5:***

1.  Take the time to fully realize your vision and your intent with "Providing for your client" BEFORE you try to get your employees on board.
2.  An environment that promotes Loyalty, Ownership, Vibrance and that rewards those who Exemplify the vision and values of the company is KEY to a prosperous business.
3.  Inspire others with your vision; you will see a whole other level of commitment from those that represent you.

## Chapter 6

# TRANSFORMING
# INTO A PROVIDER

A ssuming, up to this point, that you have made a commitment, created your vision, realized your role in facilitating that vision, and set-up your environment so that your team is excited about (and want to deliver on) the vision of the company, you are ready to continue the implementation of your new commitment of "Client Provision."

I cannot stress enough that your business will reject everything going on beyond this point IF IT HAS NOT BEEN PREPARED.

But, assuming you have followed everything up to this point, we can move on to the next phase…

If you recall the story about Bob in the beginning of this book, his primary stressors about his business were the decisions he had to make constantly, and the pressure he felt carrying the business on his shoulders. It is in this chapter that all the Bobs in the world can finally solve the riddle of how to survive—and even thrive—in a growing business. Several years ago, a fellow Christian by the name of Dr. W. Edwards Deming changed what the world viewed was possible in business and industry.

Dr. W. Edwards Deming (1900-1993), an American statistician, changed lives by developing better ways for people to work together. He derived the first philosophy and method that allowed individuals and organizations—from families and schools to government agencies and large companies—to plan and continually improve themselves, their relationships, processes, products and services. We will call this method a Customer Based Quality Management System, or, CBQMS. His philosophy is one of cooperation and continual improvement; it eradicates blame and redefines mistakes as opportunities for improvement. Through his vision and leadership, he helped rebuild the Japanese from a defeated enemy after WWII to an industrial giant in less than 50 years. It all started when the Army hired Deming to assist with the Japanese 1951 Census. While there, his expertise in quality control techniques, combined with his involvement in Japanese society, brought him an invitation from the Japanese Union of Scientists and Engineers (JUSE).[6]

As part of Japan's reconstruction efforts, the JUSE wanted an expert to teach statistical control. From June-August 1950, Deming trained hundreds of engineers, managers, and scholars in his philosophy and concepts of quality, procedure, management, and work environment cultivation. He also conducted at least one session for top management, including top Japanese industrialists (one of the more notable attendees was Akio Morita, the cofounder of Sony Corporation). Deming's message of improving quality and reducing expenses while increasing productivity and worker morale revolutionized the world and helped Japan gain market share that they never imagined.

*Photo reprinted with permission from The Deming Institute ©2015*

A number of Japanese manufacturers applied his techniques widely and experienced absolutely unheard of levels of quality and productivity. The improved quality, combined with the lowered cost, created the new international demand for Japanese products we see today.

In the years since its introduction, Deming's philosophy of continual improvement of products, services, processes, systems and people was adapted by other cultures, but rarely has been practiced in its fullness. In too many cases, especially in the United States, his philosophical principles have been reduced to promoting only continual improvement in products and services to please or delight customers, but neglecting the rest of its implementation…particularly, the cultivation of the work environment and its people. Instead of focusing on the more intangible aspects of his philosophy, as Deming advised, American companies have focused almost exclusively on the tangible products and services produced by those systems. They have often substituted measurement for management.

This is why I have made it a big part of my personal and professional mission to share the movement of Customer Based Quality Management Systems with anyone who can benefit from it. One of the biggest challenges facing a business owner is when making decisions for the direction of their business, they have very few facts. They base decisions on previous experiences (if there are any), and constantly live with doubt that they made the best decision possible. In addition, the time spent on making decisions about all parts of a company will force an owner or manager to invest time and focus into that specific segment, which in turn takes them off the focus of the entire organization.

A Customer Based Quality Management System (CBQMS) encompasses the ideology and the tools necessary for large and small organizations to make the most responsible decisions with the least amount of risk, and with the highest amount of benefit for the client. Imagine, for a moment, the relief that would come from making decisions from that position. In addition, the very foundation of most CBQMSs encourages gaining problem solving strategies from the people closest to the source, rather than from the top-down. It's about an entire business owning the deliverables, rather than just the business owner.

After 50+ years of its proof of concept, there are literally dozens of CBQMSs available for consideration. DMAIC, DMADV, Six Sigma, Lean Sigma, TQM, and ISO 9000 are just some of the most recognized ones. The one we have developed for our clients is the I.D.E.A.S model (Intention, Decision, Enhancement, Anchor, Scrutinize).

So why don't more businesses have systems like these as part of their core?

Well, usually it comes down to a few key reasons. The first and most common one is ignorance of the concept all together. Or those that have heard of it might have little knowledge or confidence on how to apply it to their own business. These systems are seen as tools for larger, more accomplished organizations. However, I have seen simplified versions of these concepts applied in self-employed professions, like real estate and financial services that get AMAZING results. If one-man operations like those can have success with this, so can you!

A second common reason business owners are reluctant to use a CBQMS may be previous negative experiences through other organizations. Total Quality Management (TQM), for example, was implemented by many American companies in the 1980's (due to the recognition of Japan's global quality dominance) with very little success. Most companies implemented the tools, but not the ideology. As a result, many companies—and even the U.S. Military—saw very little value, and for the most part it has been seen as huge disappointment.

That is why this is not chapter one, and is instead chapter five. I cannot stress enough the importance of preparing your team before implementing or even introducing a system like this. This is, ultimately, the transition from a Customer Service mindset to a Client Provision mindset in a nutshell. Being "nice" to your customer takes little to no effort. Giving them what they ask for takes very little thought or preparation. However, "Providing" for a "Client" takes a greater amount of effort and commitment all together. It is impossible to have that relationship without a CBQMS, even if you only use a simplified version of the more recognized systems.

Until an organization has accepted the vision, understands what they are trying to accomplish, and asks the question "How?", introducing a system like this and all that is involved could be potentially disastrous. Systems like these are a huge shift in how a business operates, and sometimes even how the people within the organization think. In most business environments, criticism is seen as an attack because the idea of Constant Quality Improvement (CQI) is not part of their natural environment. In essence, you have an organization that fosters PRIDE over Purpose. A matured business, instead, will see criticism as an opportunity to improve. Without the adaptation of CQI ideology, how could anyone inside your business feel comfortable bringing to the surface areas of improvement, if it involves a person or department that they value? Until criticism can be seen as a gift and opportunity to improve, rather than an offensive action, the business will never be able to meet its full potential or Purpose. The more an owner recognizes that, the more care he or she will inevitably take in its introduction. Quite often, I compare it to farming: If a person went outside in the yard and started throwing seeds on the ground at random, they would have very little success (unless it was an EXTREMELY receptive soil). On top of that, they would generally have little idea what would sprout, or when. In business, it is very much the same! In truth, to grow things in abundance it takes intent on what we want to grow, proper planning, and preparation.

Finally, the last primary reason people resist a system like this is the investment—or perceived investment—of financial and sweat resources for training and implementation. All I can say to that concern is this: in every situation I have seen it implemented correctly, it is worth it. With reductions in waste and inefficiencies, increases in market and profit, and particularly the reduction in stress of ownership and management, coupled with what they are able to deliver to their customers, there are more reasons to move forward than not. What if you have already implemented one of these systems, with the "soil" not prepared correctly, and you are now living with a functioning disaster? Well, it is never too late to get it right! Just review how we evolved to this point through the chapters, and try and recognize what steps you may have missed.

In my opinion, Christian business owners have a strategic advantage over the traditional secular companies. We already share a likeness in faith…a sort of "main drive" or "hive mind" toward the common goal of living in Christ, and being brought to Everlasting Life with Him in heaven. In that particular way, the advantage with using a CBQMS is that it is more likely to work where secular businesses have failed. We are already called to constantly improve our lives. We are already called to work collectively toward a common goal and Purpose. If a CBQMS mindset were to be applied in Christian business today, we, as a faithful people, would be absolutely unstoppable!

By fully implementing a CBQMS, you can now become the provider you always envisioned being for your clients and the one your clients always dreamed you or someone else would be to them. It can be seen in every part of your business. How you interact and determine the needs of your clients, how you meet the needs of your clients, how you deliver to your clients, how you market to your clients, how you anticipate the needs of the future, etc… I could literally go on and on about the possibilities available from such a simple enhancement and the direct and indirect benefits from implementing it. Just understand that while it may not be easy at first, every business that has integrated appropriately has seen it pay off tenfold.

***What you need to know from chapter 6:***

1. A Customer Based Quality Management System (CBQMS) encompasses the ideology and the tools necessary for large and small organizations to make the most responsible decisions with the least amount of risk, and with the highest amount of benefit for the client.
2. Systems like these are a huge shift in how a business operates, and sometimes even how the people within the organization think.
3. Christian business owners have a strategic advantage over the traditional secular companies in possible success with a CBQMS, since we already are called to constantly improve our lives and share a common goal among us.

*Chapter 7*

# THE POWER OF WISDOM

Two of my favorite stories of the Old Testament both surround King Solomon in *1 Kings 3*. The first is the story of when he was first king, at the young age of twelve. He went to Gibeon to offer sacrifices, when the Lord appeared to him in a dream and told Solomon to ask for whatever he wanted. He replied, *"7 Now, LORD my God, you have made your servant king in place of my father David. But I am only a little child and do not know how to carry out my duties. 8 Your servant is here among the people you have chosen, a great people, too numerous to count or number. 9 So give your servant a discerning heart to govern your people and to distinguish between right and wrong. For who is able to govern this great people of yours?"*

The second story is the most famous one about King Solomon. It was the wise ruling he gave when two women came before him that lived in the same house, and both had babies of similar age. One of the babies had died in the night, and the two women were fighting over which was the real mother. King Solomon settled the dispute by calling for the child to be cut in two. The first woman, moved with love for her son, begged that his life be spared, even if it meant the other woman would get him. The second woman spoke up, saying that the ruling was just, for neither one would get the baby. King Solomon declared, "Give the living baby to the first woman. Do not kill him; she is his mother."

While the second story is an impressive demonstration of the depth of the king's wisdom, to me, the first story is the greatest. To ask for wisdom regarding every decision was what he believed would make him the greatest leader for his people, even at a tender age, and it shows that wisdom was with him even before the Lord granted it.

As business owners and managers, we are asked constantly to make decisions of every kind. Quite often, those decisions affect many people, including those who work for us, the families that depend on that income, and the clients we provide for. So why is it we feel compelled to make such decisions without fully understanding what we are trying to accomplish, what collateral impact it may have, and what a successful decision would look like?

Try to recall the last time you made a decision for your business. How much of it was made based on factual information collected, sorted, and presented, with a clear idea of what a successful decision would look like?

By the way, measuring success should be a lot more than determining if a job was profitable or at least broke even. Using profit as a measurement does not reflect the true intent of Client Provision, or our faith.

Generally what happens when making decisions, instead, is a lot of opinion, past experience, and intuition. While these assets can serve a great deal in the decision making process, they also hold the risk of making us fall into the same mistakes over and over, stagnating the potential of a business.

In this chapter, we will introduce the advantages of automation, systemization, and having the critical data to make strategic decisions rather than reactionary ones.

Strategic decisions are made when we have a clear intent and the information we need to make the best informed decision available. In the previous chapter, we discussed the importance of researching and implementing a CBQMS. It is the only solution to fulfilling your commitment to your client's short term and long term needs. In this chapter, we will discuss how these tools can specifically improve every part of your business including quality, consistency, marketing, efficiency, and profitability. But again, this is assuming that you have a clear vision for how you will be providing for your client, you have formatted that vision in a way your team understands it, and that your team is supportive of the mission. If you skip to this chapter and try to implement these tools without the environment in place, the cost of implementing will be tenfold, and the effectiveness will be greatly reduced. This is about an entire organization sharing the same passion for providing, and always searching for ways to provide at a higher level. While the benefits of implementing this type of system are too many to name, there are some that are GAME CHANGERS for your business.

The first game changer is the fundamental change in the culture of your business. The core part of all these systems is the empowerment of the workforce to discover and improve quality. As I mentioned in previous chapters, most businesses operate in a top-down quality model. The standards are set and held by the top of the organization, and slowly dissipate as you go down. With CBQMS systems, the entire organization is empowered with the authority to maintain and improve quality, and as a result, management has more time to innovate and plan rather than keeping up minimum standards.

The second game changer is the ability to make informed decisions. The fundamental premise of a CBQMS is data collection and analysis. When making decisions for a business, at times, our experiences and intuition can betray us. Times change, our perception is different, and we may not always have the same people in place to implement the new course of action. Using our experience, while coupling it with factual information, increases the likelihood of success and saves resources spent on guesswork. In addition, a CBQMS model provides a tool to see how well our solution has worked, and whether it has been fully implemented.

Another challenge that business owners face constantly is identifying the specific weak areas of their business. If you have a problem in your sales division, is it because of the amount of leads, quality of leads, or conversion rate? If you are having problems with the profitability of jobs is it because it was bid too low, not organized appropriately, or not managed properly? If you are having trouble with timely delivery, is it because of manufacturing timelines or shipping practices? Identifying and tracking Key Performance Indicators (KPIs) can help identify the major cause of an issue, while also providing a starting place to get down to the root cause of the problem. This saves a great amount of frustration, but also helps prevent businesses from making changes that might make a problem even worse.

Dr. Deming often said, "Uncontrolled variation is the enemy of quality." A core principle of every CBQMS is creating consistent outputs to reduce or even eliminate the need for quality checkpoints. The theory is, if a system is put together and implemented, the result should be consistent. This allows the next link in the chain to deliver consistent outputs at optimal time and efficiency, thereby ultimately producing at a high rate and high level of quality. In addition, we rely less on the skills of the people inside the system, and more on the system itself, which reduces a great amount of stress, anxiety, and costly mistakes. Leadership can then focus more on managing the process, knowing that a well-managed process will produce the results they are seeking.

Finally, the last game changer is scalability. Once a process is in place for any part of a business, you now have the ability to grow your business to any level of production you see fit. If you want to increase sales, you need only to increase the KPI of a particular area of the process and your sales will increase. If you want to prepare your business for higher production, you need only to examine the areas that will become choke points, and focus resources in that area. Your business can finally become a vehicle by which there are no limitations on its potential, and fulfill whatever God has planned for its Purpose.

What is most upsetting about this topic, for me, is that this information has been available for more than a generation, but still has not become a regular part of how we operate our business. The biggest stresses of any business, nine times out of ten, can be eliminated with the implementation of what is in the chapters of this book... and it really isn't that difficult. Through strategic decisions made up of clear intent, Divine assistance, and factual information, we can use wisdom as an asset in growing our business.

*What you need to know from chapter 7:*

1.  CBQMS creates "game changers" in our business: a fundamental culture shift, the ability to make informed decisions, and scalability.
2.  Through strategic decisions made up of clear intent, divine assistance, and factual information, we can use wisdom as an asset in our business.

# End of Section 2

It has been such a blessing sharing the "Client Provision" implementation system with you. Through my extensive individual and corporate coaching, I have seen firsthand the tremendous positive impact this system has on businesses, ownership, corporate leaders, their teams, and those the business is called to provide for. It has been very fulfilling and gives true meaning to what I do every day. It is up to you now to impact the world in the way that only you can. To help you in your journey I have included an outline of all the phases along with links to all the books and documents I recommend in *God's Business Fast Action Guide*. You can obtain your copy at www.GodsBusinessTheBook.com.

There is still one final leg to your journey. Section 3 challenges many of the beliefs you likely have about your business and your role as the owner. This section serves as your final piece of the puzzle. This section clarifies what to do when you as the owner of your business are ready to embrace the evolutions of your business, and don't know where to start.

Download God's Business Fast Action Guide
www.godsbusinessthebook.com

Section 3

# SHORTENING YOUR WALK THROUGH THE DESERT

# INTRODUCTION

The final section of this book is comprised of the most common conquerable obstacles plaguing business today. Unlike the previous chapters that highlighted how to deliver a higher standard of how you provide for your clients, the three concepts in this section have to do with the habits or beliefs that YOU HAVE AS A BUSINESS OWNER that are holding your business back. Client Provision for most Christian business owners and organizations feels like a very natural transition, but in this final section, when challenging some of the beliefs that got you to where you are, it can be a little harder. All I suggest is to just open your heart and mind a little while moving on, and I promise what you need to hear will ring through.

Few businesses have the blessing of standing the test of time. Great intentions and great people come and go… some lasting a short spell, and others lasting a generation or two. So, what is it that separates a business that has been around for 100 years from that of a business that has been struggling to hang on only after 15 years? It isn't growth; because many of us have seen wildly successful businesses disappear practically overnight. It isn't the economy, because any business that has lasted 100 years has been through more than one struggling economy. In many cases, it isn't even specific to industry. Even though several companies that have lasted that long are in similar industries (financial services is one that comes to mind) there are plenty more that are not. The truth is, there are many reasons, but none of them are more important than this:

The long term success of a business is dependent on the love for its client over the love for the product or service it provides.

As mentioned in previous chapters, the greatest advantage we as Christian business owners have is that the fundamental parts of our faith evoke us to always have compassion for those we provide for. This means the transition from a focus on what we do, to whom we do it for—and the needs that they have—can be that much easier.

## Chapter 8

# FALLING IN LOVE WITH YOUR PRODUCT IS KILLING YOUR BUSINESS

E arlier in the book, I highlighted the Studebaker's business evolution from a successful wheelbarrow[5] manufacturer to the premiere provider of automobiles. From their founding in 1852, until their final closure in the 1960's, they were touted as the icon of quality and reliability in everything they did. Some could argue that using a business that ultimately closed would not be the best example. To that I would say, their demise was not due to the commitment to provide the automobile, but rather, other decisions made toward the end of their existence.

However, for those who wish for a more "suitable" illustration, another great example of longevity can be found in the ADT security company. Founded and formed in 1874, as a collaboration of over 50 telegraph delivery companies (American District Telegraph), this organization made themselves aware of the world changing around them. As the need for telegraphs declined due to the growing popularity of the telephone, they discovered a new underserved market in providing fire and security alarms, leveraging the new technology of the telephone. As a result, ADT is still the largest provider of security services in the United States and Canada, with over 6 million active customers. While these first two examples are companies that were formed and forged over 100 years ago, they remain present-day examples of this principle.

McDonald's is another corporation that comes to mind that has found a way to focus on their clients rather than their product. Most people are familiar with the story of how Ray Kroc was able to purchase the rights to franchising the McDonald brother's hamburger stand in the 1950's.[7] What isn't as widely discussed is how McDonald's has been able to maintain itself as one of the premiere franchise opportunities, even after almost 60 years. Through the identifying of the needs of their patrons worldwide, and then adapting their menus to fit their needs, McDonalds has become one of the most recognizable brands in the world. In addition, here in the United States over the last 20 years, McDonald's has made several changes to their menu options to include healthier options as we enter an age of new health awareness. While people believe that this is something new, McDonald's has always evolved with the needs of their clientele. It has been the commitment to understanding their client, rather than focusing on the burgers and fries they started with, that has helped them prosper and endure. As you can see from the above examples, companies that are successful long term follow the same patterns. The ones that are built to last all evolve with their clients. So why is it that so many other businesses struggle to do the same thing?

While there is still a great debate whether independent businesses or franchises have a higher rate of long term success, if you were to look at the strategic advantages of franchises in comparison to start-up businesses, the list is considerable. There are many contributing factors, including automated systems, financial commitment, and industry. Something that also is a major contributor to the longevity of a franchise is the attachment they have with their product or service in comparison to their independent counterparts. A franchisee could really care less if the corporation changed a menu item or discontinued a product, as long as there was a reason for it, and some means of restitution. On the other hand, an independent business told that their product or service— that he or she has delivered for so many years— is now obsolete and no longer acceptable, would often feel a blow to how they personally define themselves.

While this may be only one example, there are countless others that highlight one very true fact of business:

When we identify our business too closely to our product or service, we potentially sign the death certificate for our business.

## The S-Curve

The dangers in having too close a relationship with a product or service is that, at some point, the demand—or at least the profitability—of any and every product or service will run its course. To fully understand this concept, we can use an illustration below simulating a principle known as the S-Curve.

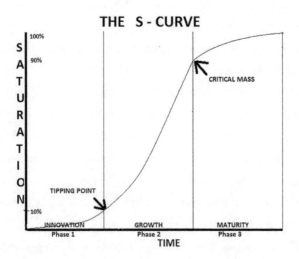

The S-Curve is a mathematical graph demonstrating the life cycle of most products and services. The curve itself is made up of three phases: the innovation phase (1-10% market saturation), the growth phase (10-90% market saturation), and the maturity phase (90-100% market saturation). One of the most profound parts of the S-Curve is that during the growth phase, 80 percent of the specified product, service, or other "measurable" is adapted into the potential market. What makes this even more surprising is that the time periods of each phase are, historically, directly proportionate to each other. This means the amount of time a product takes to go from 1 percent to 10 percent adaptation is directly proportionate to the amount of time it will take that same product to go from 10 percent to 90 percent. The final third of the curve is also directly proportionate, as adaptation hits "critical mass" and the final 90 to 100 percent catch up. Over history, the S- Curve has been illustrated countless times in industries, specific products, and technology. One of the more recent examples has been the S-Curve of the cell phone. National towers for cellular service were first introduced in the early 80's. From 1981 to 1996, the first fifteen years of their existence, cellular subscriptions rose to a little over 33 million in the United States. From 1996 to 2011 (another 15 years), cellular subscriptions rose from a little over 33 million to over 300 million, with a just below 90 percent saturation. While we are still waiting for the final 10 percent to adapt, cell phones will most likely be in the high 90th percentile— if not 100 percent— by the year 2026.[8]

If you were to ask any company when the best opportunity for profitability was in the cell phone industry, I can promise you it was between the years of 1995 and 2010. I could go on in great detail about other industries that have grown based on this principle, but rather than take up too much of your time, I invite you to research the principle on your own.

So what does this have to do with your business?

There is a difference between the S-Curve of a product or service, and that of an industry. While the cell phone product has hit critical mass, the communication industry has not. Inside of the communication industry, we have evolved from telegraphs, to telephones, to cell phones, to the use of mobile devices like the iPad and tablets. Within the industry as a whole, there have been several S-Curves. But some businesses, like AT&T (which is another company that has lasted over 100 years), realized that they were in the communications business, and not the wired telephone business that it started as in the 1880's. Businesses that are able to recognize the rising tide of innovation have an immeasurable advantage. There are changes happening constantly in the products and services, as well as in the way that they are distributed and marketed. If a business is able to recognize the wave at the tipping point of its growth phase, and continue to recognize the next wave before the current one hits critical mass, they will be in a position of unlimited profitability and growth. It is when we are "married" to what we do—or the way that we do things—that puts us in a position of vulnerability and obsolescence. Another danger facing businesses, due to the information age, is the rate of adaptation inside the S-Curve. The S-Curves of the early 20th century, like the telephone and the automobile, took more than a generation to get through all three phases. However, the S-Curve of the credit card and the cell phone took only one generation. Fast forwarding to today, the S-Curves of the internet, Facebook, and mobile devices are taking just a little more than a decade. This means if we, as businesses, are not on the lookout for changing tides, it may blow right past us—or even worse—trample right over us. The old saying, "If it's not broken, don't fix it!" can spell death for a business, now more than ever. In previous times, businesses were able to recover from late adaptation because the S-Curve, itself, gave them enough time to figure out what was going on. Today, however, there is very little opportunity to make up ground lost due to having your head in the sand.

**Marriage is a Commitment that Transcends Comfort**
After spending some time on the benefits of understanding your industry and falling in love with your client, let's discuss the specific dangers of "marrying" your product or service. As a husband in a successful relationship of over fifteen years, I am huge supporter of the blessing marriage can be. Due to the success my wife and I have had, I am often approached by people wanting to know our "secret." Some are considering the covenant themselves, others are early in their marriage and want guidance, and others are having challenges and want to find ways to improve their relationship. One of my favorite points to make is, "You are marrying the woman, my friend, not the flesh." What this basically means is the commitment you are making needs to be able to stand the test that time will give, especially when the commitment is made with the intention to last beyond physical, mental, or

financial health. By committing to our whole partner and not just a part of them, we prepare our relationship to last a lifetime. The joy and satisfaction of the holy union of marriage is life-long, and should be represented in everything that we do. As a matter of consequence, something that also needs to be considered before the union is that marriage carries with it certain blind spots and specific commitments. So if our intention is to commit for life, we must ensure that we are prepared to fulfill that commitment for a *lifetime*.

In business, this comparison highlights the difference between marrying your product and marrying your client. The product, like flesh, at some point will wither away with time. However, as long as there are people on Earth, your business will always have someone to provide for. While there are many benefits to marriage, there are several dangers when married to the wrong element in business (or in life!) that can prove disastrous.

**Blind to Faults** – One of the greatest blessings—but also biggest dangers—of marriage is the fact that you become blind to faults. These rose colored glasses act as a blessing due to the innocent bliss they create. This can be a problem, though, when we turn a blind eye to things that can potentially put us in harm's way. In business, this could mean you become blind to the cycle your business is in. It could mean that you become blind to the way you market your business, or even the way you produce the product. In some cases, it may be the people who represent the business we are blind to, at the sacrifice of the relationships of our clients.

Focusing on our clients, instead of our business, allows us to make the decisions that we have to in order to keep a healthy thriving relationship. I would also like to take the opportunity to clarify the difference between providing for your clients and committing to one particular type of client. There may be situations where marrying a certain client can be harmful. After some time, you may no longer be the best provider of your product or service for a specific consumer and/or segment. Especially after critical mass, there may be more beneficial options for clients you previously provided for. The reason is that businesses, at some point, may evolve to where it is no longer in the best interest of either party to continue providing for specific clients due to skill, costs, or evolution of the product or service. It is at that point a business must be aware of their limitations, and be honest with their clients and themselves.

**Faithfulness** – When committing to anything, one of the core principles is to be faithful. In marriage, when we commit to the rest of our natural life with our spouse, this also means we commit to hold them above all others. In business, this can also happen after committing to a specific part of our business. If there is too strong of an alignment to a specific product, service, or way of doing things, there is a risk of guilt when looking the other way. What this means for a business is they risk making changes too slowly, or they may disregard beneficial opportunities. However, when the commitment lies with the client, our focus is on the providing of their needs over our own. This means we are always exploring ways to stay faithful to our commitment to them.

**Stop Trying to Impress** –Another inevitability of a maturing relationship is the courtship. When someone marries the flesh, and the flesh begins to subside, the courtship usually goes with it. Far too often, we have witnessed relationships lose fire because what they have committed to has passed with time. The two parties become complacent and bored, and very little effort is made to engage or enjoy each other. In business, when married to a specific product or service, we stop trying to find ways to keep the "what we do" fresh and exciting because "what we do" begins losing its luster. The relationship that we have becomes a monotonous 9 to 5 commitment, with very little flare or excitement. On the other hand, a client is everlasting, and the relationship never ages. As the S-Curve evolves, the relationship is made new again with no end in sight. You continue to court each other, because the love is renewed with every delivery, and you are always seeking ways to impress. A great example of this concept is the "new" Apple. After several years of disaster, Apple brought Steve Jobs back, and with his leadership they turned a company on the brink of bankruptcy back to being one of the most successful turnaround stories of our time. What Jobs discovered when he got there was that executives believed they were in the business of personal computers. However, due to the S-Curve of the PC market and the tight grip Microsoft had on software, there was no room or opportunity for Apple to compete in that market. It was Steve

Jobs who made them see they were in the business of "media entertainment," and that there was far more opportunity in that segment. As a result, this brought on ITunes, the IPod, the IPhone, and the IPad, and really changed the landscape of the industry. He continually courted his client by always giving them something more than before, and was unwavering in finding ways to do just that. When you understand the business you are really in, and the clients you really provide for, magical things can happen. Things that were once unimaginable become reality, and the love that is shared is unwavering.

**Emotion vs. Logic** – The final blessing —and danger— of a marriage is the way we make decisions. When we are in love, we sometimes cannot see the forest for the trees. We end up making decisions that no sane or logical person would make. While most people would argue that we always make decisions based on the most accurate application of the facts, the truth is, we don't. We are emotional beings, and will almost always make our decisions with emotion first, and logic second. Consider decisions you have made, for example, that may have favored your business, rather than your client. You may be amazed if you sat down and thought about it.

If you have paid attention throughout this book, you already know how much I believe the core concepts of everything that has been written is directly from our faith. In this specific section, this realization rings truer than almost any of the others. It is said constantly throughout the New Testament that a focus on others over ourselves brings with it immeasurable riches. One way to receive those riches, while still here on Earth, is through the commitment of "focusing on others" through your business. In doing so, your clients will be witnesses of your commitment and reward you accordingly.

## Chapter 9

# WORKING THE JOBSITE IS KILLING YOUR BUSINESS

I t's tough letting others represent your business when you have worked so hard building it. However, the only way for your business to achieve its glory is to empower others with the means to help.

When delving into this topic, it is hard to ignore the great internal conflict most business owners have. In essence, by separating themselves from the roles that they excel at in their business, and forcing them into roles that they may or may not be comfortable with invites doubt, anxiety, and above all else, fear. Those of us who have built our reputation and business on our name naturally feel compelled to protect that image... and justifiably so. However, restricting the graces that God wishes to bestow on us and those who we provide for, based on our own insecurities, is not what we are called to do. As I have mentioned previously, I felt called to share the vision of this book with my Christian brothers and sisters, just as much as I felt that those who have the opportunity to read it are called to take action. For far too long, we have been convinced that we are alone in our travels, and for whatever reason, we have accepted that we are not the person who can build a business nationally or even internationally. I promise you that if you are not that man or woman today, you can be tomorrow if you choose to be. All it takes is a decision about who we are able to be, with Christ's help, and the knowledge that we are called to do His works on Earth while we are here. After doing so, you will quickly realize that in order to fulfill our mission, our role in our business must evolve, and that which we feared was the only thing holding us back from the greatness God had planned for us.

We are all ultimately under the Good Shepherd during our time here on Earth; however, we are called to "feed his lambs and tend his sheep (**John 21:15–19**)." What I celebrate most about this calling is the relationship between The Shepherd and the Flock. With its implied symbiosis, there is a deeper understanding that the Shepherd and Flock are equally dependent on each other, and as a result, neither holds entire power over the other. For the Shepherd, the Flock offers critical resources such as economic value, environmental control, and subsistence. As for the Flock, they are dependent on the Shepherd for food and protection from predators and themselves.

Likewise, in the business world, there is a symbiotic relationship between Employee and Employer. The Employer is entirely dependent on the Employee to fulfill the vision of the company through their actions, ideas, and hands. At the same time, the Employee is dependent on the Employer for compensation that puts food on their tables, but also for the Employer's knowledge and wisdom to keep the company and its Employees healthy for the long term. So what happens when a Flock has no Shepherd?

***Imminent Danger.***

There is a reason why only 25% of businesses fail after the 1st year, but over 70% of businesses fail after 10 years, and only 1% of that failure is tied to neglect, fraud, or disaster.[9]

It is because there is critical danger in playing the same role we did in the beginning of our business as our Flock continues to grow. As a company grows, the increased numbers of opportunities are also followed by increased likelihood of hazards. An owner who is working on the jobsite with his crew, or doing project management, cannot protect his company any more than a member of the Flock can protect the herd… neither have the opportunity to see the lay of the land for what lies ahead. While the evolution from being part of the Flock to becoming the Shepherd does not happen overnight, it is important that we truly assess where we are, and determine if it provides for the needs of the business. We can then put together a plan to evolve our role, and put that plan into action. In this chapter is a brief description of the three different roles that are filled in your business. An owner, at times, may fill all of these roles at one point or another in their business life, and depending on the stage of the business, it may be necessary. However, the risk comes in when an owner does not have a balance reflective of the needs of the business, and finds themselves unable or unwilling to accept the role necessary to fill the vacuum left by growth.

I think this is one of the hardest transitions for most small business owners... especially those who started a company based on their skills or trade. For years, they have built relationships and leveraged opportunities based on their name, and it is extremely difficult to risk allowing others to represent it. In addition, what aren't discussed as often are the benefits that come directly from filling this role. For people who work with their hands, there is a certain amount of satisfaction that comes from seeing something manifest from their labors. The work gets performed their way and by their standards if they are directly involved in managing its completion. Coupled with more control of the individual job and less anxiety, it easy to understand why this can become a plateau for many owners.

However, anyone who spends the majority of their time in this role knows that the biggest drawback is the stunted growth. Bottlenecks get formed because the leadership of the company is trying to do more than one person is capable. When attempting to branch out, things can get overwhelming fast, and in many cases work quality suffers, either by employees or by their own hands. The business becomes stagnant, and it can become difficult to attract and retain great talent because there is very little opportunity for growth. In essence, they have built themselves a really great job that they can set the terms for, but it also comes with a whole lot more liability. In addition, while working beside the rest of the Flock, they have stunted their growth just because of their presence. You are either their friend or their boss and neither one allows them to grow professionally (more on this later).

**The Herding Dog (Manager)**
At some point, an owner evolves to the "Herding Dog" role in their business, and while this is an upgrade from the previous role, it can also be misleading. They begin to delegate tasks and responsibilities, and excel in getting the most out of the Flock. However, a Herding Dog could never play the role of the Shepherd completely....like having an understanding of the hazards of the land, where to find the most plentiful pastures, and the ability to groom the Flock. While the Flock understands and responds to the Herding Dog, they recognize his limitations and still respond to the voice of their Shepherd, above all. In business, there is a big difference between being a "Leader" and a "Manager." A friend of mine explained it very well

a long time ago with this story. There are many different versions, but this is my favorite:

A crew of men was in the jungle, trying to get to camp. After several hours the leader realized that no one had gotten bearings for quite some time. So he alerted the manager and said, "Hey, wouldn't it be a good idea to climb to the top of one of these trees and see where we are going?" The Manager replied, "Sure, you can do that, but we are going to keep cutting down here while you go up." It took almost an hour to climb, but then after the climber was able to get a good view, he realized that the crew had gotten off track and was going in the wrong direction. He called down, "Hey we are cutting the WRONG WAY!" In reply, the manager yells up, "I'M NOT WORRIED ABOUT THAT, WE ARE MAKING GREAT TIME DOWN HERE!"

Managers are task-oriented, and for a good reason. Their responsibilities are to complete their objective with the utmost quality, efficiency, and professionalism. However, what comes with a laser focus is, of course, A LASER FOCUS! They can often times miss the bigger picture, and not see how their actions are affecting the overall objective. Now, having a Manager mindset may not seem all that bad. For example, you still maintain much of the control of the project, which means the anxiety of separating and allowing people to do the work isn't fully realized. Your labor responsibilities most likely are reduced, and you are able to fill in where needed without other parts of the work getting neglected. The company is able to grow in many areas because you are able to task others. You are also able to establish some posture, which allows for standards to be conveyed and expected by others. You are still interacting with people in a position of authority, you may have no labor responsibilities, and you may be coordinating multiple jobs. While the differences between the Shepherd and the Herding Dog can be confusing for many business owners, one of the main indicators is the mentality the owner has while the work is being performed.

As mentioned before, with a focus still on the task at hand, Managers are doers and have little time for looking ahead or looking behind. As a result, they are unable to provide the company with the necessary resources for stability and growth. A Manager is satisfied when the work is getting done, regardless of the personal resources needed to complete it. So even if they must get on the machine, or run the saw, or complete the admin, they are perfectly satisfied as long as a hard day's work is represented by something to show for it. A Leader (Shepherd), on the other hand, looks at scalability. If every job was completed this way, would it be optimal, sustainable, and representative of the vision of the company? How is it affecting other parts of the company, as far as how they are able to perform with the output delivered? Is there a better way to get this done by maximizing our available resources, or are there opportunities to obtain new resources that would have allowed us to leverage our current resources more? These only highlight some of the mentality differences, however, there are many more.

**The Shepherd (Leader)**

When the owner finally takes on the role of the Shepherd for the majority of their time, amazing things can happen. The Flock is well protected and well supported, which allows for limitless growth. The organization is now ready to meet its full potential, and develops an insatiable appetite to grow the company and vision. This all happens because the "Shepherd" is able to focus on delivering on the needs of the organization, rather than completing the specific tasks at hand. These needs include:

- The Vision
- Belief that the Vision can be accomplished
- An Environment and Culture the business can flourish in
- The Tools needed to implement the Vision
- A Plan and System by which they can obtain it

(Look familiar?)

Another trait of the Shepherd is that they understand they can't—and shouldn't—do everything all on their own. It is quite common for the Flock or the Herding Dog to make the decision to do something themselves, rather than develop others and be patient while they are learning it. It is an instinctual action, and for them it doesn't represent any negative consequences. However, the Shepherd isn't focused just on the task or job at hand. They realize that every action or reaction can carry with it an unrealized consequence in the future. Problems like bottlenecking, stagnant skill development, inconsistent quality standards, or even unintentional precedents can be the result of owning the mentality of "If it needs to be done, I am the one to do it." Instead, deciding on a standard and recruiting or training others to meet that standard becomes the primary focus. For the Shepherd, it is about consistency and scalability. There is very little need to know how to do everything. Instead, it is about knowing where to find someone who can, or knowing the source where they can develop their team to be able to do it. They also realize if they are the ones always doing it, no one else will ever need to learn how to.

### The True "Peter Principle"

Laurence J. Peter wrote a book titled, *The Peter Principle: Why Things Always Go Wrong*, in 1969. Interestingly enough, since its publishing, the interpretation of "Peter" has become associated with the disciple Peter in many renditions, even though the book was never intended to align itself with the saint. In *The Peter Principle*, Laurence Peter describes the many problems with hierarchical structures in business. The first of which (and most importantly) is that successful people will always be promoted from competent positions to the point where they will reach a position of incompetence. At that point, the system will do everything in its power to maintain the hierarchical structure. This includes management setting lower parts of the hierarchy up to fail to reduce the chance of promotion. In addition, lower parts find themselves bypassing incompetent management to fulfill requirements to minimize the damage done by their incompetence. The parallel between these principles and Peter is established when Christ recruits Peter, a great fishermen of his day, to become a "fisher of men" for the Lord. Through all four of the Gospels, you hear about the struggles of Peter's feeling of inadequacy. He allows his instincts to overcome his better judgment, and he constantly challenged Christ to prove who he was. Even worse, the man Christ picked to "build His church" on was the man who so vehemently denied him during his persecution in the square. It would seem, on the outset, that this fisherman who was "promoted" to be a fisher of men was incapable of fulfilling that duty.

My biggest concerns with these associations are:

1. The original text was written as a satire, and though it does have some relevant ideals, it was never intended to be a standard to compare to… especially not with Saint Peter of the Bible.
2. When being compared to the Biblical Peter, many people neglect to finish the story. Most importantly, Peter's eventual evolution to the leader Christ saw him to be and how he was literally the man the modern church was built on.

So how does this distinction relate to growing leadership in your business?

I would argue that Peter's competence was not realized due to lack of necessity much more than lack of ability. Christ knew what Peter was capable of well before anyone else did, including himself. Is there any question that Christ knew exactly what Peter was going to do every step of the way? Even the night before he was to be crucified, he knew exactly how many times Peter would deny him. It probably wasn't until that moment that Peter realized exactly how much Christ actually knew about him. The truth is, Peter wasn't able to realize what he was capable of until he had to, which was when Christ was no longer there, and the vacuum of leadership was created. Similarly, your very presence at the worksite stunts the growth of your leadership, because leadership will not fully develop until it has to.

One of the main reasons leadership does not develop without a vacuum is that the highest present authority dictates the standard that work is to be completed to, regardless of the specific instruction of immediate leadership. I have personally witnessed—on more than one occasion— when a higher-tiered manager actually undercut the higher quality standard of designated leadership in front of the crew, and without discussion or notification. Now, whether the standard was appropriate or not, the authority of the designated person is questioned for the remainder of the higher authority's presence, possibly for the remainder of the job or the indefinite future. Another reason leadership requires a vacuum to grow is that the majority of people will not question the authority of a higher-tiered person out of respect or fear. They are afraid of making mistakes and taking the initiative to try things in a different way. This includes improving the current procedure by which the work is completed, or even actively pursuing ways to improve. Most managers are happy when work is completed the way they would do it themselves, and the people under them know it.

So how does your presence stunt growth? The fact of the matter is that people know they risk more by challenging the owner, than by diverting all authority to them. This reality would be fine if the owner wanted to be in charge of every part of their business. However, we have already discussed the results that limitation can bring. This can be avoided by designating competent authority, and by diverting all outputs within their control. By doing so, we now allow our Leaders and Managers inside our business to have the space to fully realize their gifts and potential. So while it may be true, to some extent, that people will eventually be promoted to a position that they are not capable of, with the right environment, support, tools, and space, they may be groomed to be more.

**Power is in the Path**
One of the other challenges that derives from a Shepherd acting as one of the Flock or as a Herding Dog is the balance of power, or more appropriately, *a lack* of power. A growing, sustainable business must have the appropriate balance between all of its functions, including Sales, Accounting, and Production. There are times in the evolution and growth

of a business where one of these areas may be slightly more potent than the others, but in a healthy company balance always gets restored. One of the more common ailments of a stagnant or volatile company is due to the path of the ownership. In short, the power of the company is enriched in the path of the Ownership. When an owner comes from a Production background, all of his or her beliefs, motivations, and actions have a tendency to be biased and based on the scope of production. This may include challenges with quality, consistency, systems, or client communication among other things. If the owner comes from a Sales path, challenges and opportunities are observed from the scope of sales. This may include overpromising to clients, a belief that "more sales fixes everything," or the lack of appreciation for the work done by others. If the Owner comes from an Accounting or Administration background, there is a tendency towards overcompensating rigidness, systems, and risk aversion. Of all the complications of a growing developing business, the owner not incorporating the balance of power is one of the most severe. A Shepherd is able to separate themselves from the flock and see how each entity is able to contribute to the success—or the detriment—of the others. Growth is about a balanced ecosystem, and that can only come from an appreciation of all its parts from the top.

## Life as a Shepherd

The hardest part of the transition for many Herding Dogs to the role of Shepherd is the doubt they must cope with on a daily basis. Before, they proved their skill or ability with physical representations like numbers or structures, and now as a leader, proof is less obvious to everyone else. A Shepherd's proof is in the way that a team is performing and the pastures that they lay ahead for them. While a Herding Dog or the Flock has a definite beginning and end that represents their accomplishments, a Shepherd is measured by what is and what will be, and rarely has something physical to show for it other than the success of the flock.

Managers are more commonly given duties and assignments that fit within their scope of abilities, while Leaders are constantly asked to seek out answers that are not readily known. This is why a Shepherd—more than anyone else—needs to have a relationship with God like no other. Being the Shepherd for your business means having a lot of faith while dealing with the uncertainty about what lies ahead. The doubt may never fully go away, we are human after all, but we can make ourselves more capable by being more selective with the company we keep, especially with having God the closest one by our side.

## Chapter 10

# GIVING OUT RAISES IS
# KILLING YOUR BUSINESS

*"PETER! Put your sword back in its place! For all who take hold of the sword will die by the sword..."*
**Matthew 26:52**

So many core principles of our faith can be derived from this short passage of the Gospel, written during the events of the Passion of Christ. What is so magnificent about this part of scripture is how it can transcend to every part of our lives. Anytime we reach for a weapon, ANY weapon, the same weapon can be used to our demise.

In business, this is prevalent in our management skills, leadership skills, sales skills, etc... but probably is most prevalent in how we deal with securing our team. We constantly "take up arms" with our checkbooks when attracting and retaining employees. It is this constant battle between what the market perceives is "fair" compensation, and what our competitors are willing to pay to attract our talent. In essence, we are all using the same "sword," and at the end of the day, it provides very little value or stability for growth, neither for the employee nor the businesses that employ them. There is no question that we must physically compensate our people based on their value to our mission, and based on their specific needs. However, if our commitment goes only as far as the dollar, so will theirs...

In this chapter, we will explore the less often considered value we can provide, and discover ways that we can use it as leverage in competing with others for talent.

### Christian Business Ownership

One of the most common concerns I address with business owners is the workforce of the twenty-first century. It is no secret that with the evolution of information and technology, we have taken great strides in many areas. But in some ways, it has been at the expense of what can be described as very basic work and life skills. In addition, the pendulum has swayed in the opposite direction when it comes to the right of the worker, and businesses have to be more cautious than ever when dealing with their team. It is imperative therefore that we, as business owners, develop our skills as "Shepherds" and provide our people with the best opportunity to succeed. We no longer live in a time where people are just happy to have a job, and satisfied with a hard day's work. They are dynamic, and desire more from their labors. We also cannot ignore the fact that due to our Social Welfare System, the threat of being out of work no longer is a deterrent. Maybe there will be a time when society will come closer to the center, but in the meantime, a thriving business needs to know a way to leverage what is available to them.

A new approach that has developed over the last generation or so is the "Hire Slow, Fire Fast" mentality. With modern transportation and communication, businesses have a larger group to retrieve from, and should take advantage of the large pool of qualified people available today. However, as older generations leave the workforce, and younger ones become the primary pool, "finding" the right person will get harder and "developing" the right person will be the necessity. But is this really something that is entirely new?

### He Qualifies the Called

One of my favorite Christian philosophies is, "God doesn't call the qualified, He qualifies the called." Over the years, people have expanded on this philosophy, and have used examples to prove the position. One of the more entertaining ways is the story of The Angel and Balaam's Donkey illustrated in **Numbers 22: 22-35**. While the Scripture would be much too long to lay out here, **verse 28** reads:

*"And the LORD opened the mouth of the donkey, and she said to Balaam, "What have I done to you, that you have struck me these three times?"*

You see that God will work with what He has. Throughout scripture so many of our stories were of men and women called despite their humanity or transgressions. Peter had a temper and denied Christ, David had an affair and tried to cover it up with murder, Jonah ran from God. Isaiah preached naked for three years, John the Baptist ate bugs and had second thoughts about the very Messiah he baptized. Abraham was old, and Lazarus was dead.

That pretty much sums it up. If God, Himself, realizes the best person is not found, but is instead *developed and motivated*, what makes us think that the focus of our efforts shouldn't be the same? Your business has a great opportunity when it becomes an incubator for developing talent and gains a reputation that attracts others. While there are some positions that require a great amount of expertise and education, how much time do you spend in your business grooming your people to be able to take advantage of the growth happening in your company? If your company needs a social media expert, train one! If your company absolutely needs an in house marketing expert, train one! With the suitable type of environment, the appropriate educational resources, and the right type of motivation, there is no limit to the amount of qualified people you would have for positions in your business, because you would have made them! For far too long, we have depended on the "dollar" to motivate those around us, whether out of reward or punishment. As a result, our skills as "Qualifiers of Men" have gotten soft, and we have ended up in the situation we have today because of our own actions. Regardless of the reasons behind this self-created challenge, it is even more important than ever for companies to promote a "winning culture." If a company—big or small—is unable to move beyond physical compensation to motivate its employees, it is destined to continue to lose good people to the competition, and deal with sluggish and uninspired production.

A question that I often get is, "When it comes to motivating our team, what else is there?"

There are so many things that motivate people:

Money, friendship, benefits, security, opportunity, and more!

As a result, there are all kinds of reasons that people choose to work for (and stay with) a company. However, certain motivators can be more potent and even unique... motivators, that when compared to others, are more fulfilling for the short and long term. When we are able to apply higher level motivators, we separate ourselves from the majority of other employers, thereby attracting and retaining a better quality of people. In doing so, we secure for our company the best available talent to deliver on our commitment to our clients. This is a far reach from the employer paying just enough for people not to quit, and employees working just hard enough not to get fired.

Below are the Four Levels of Motivators:

- *(Level 1) Material* – Pay, Benefits, Vacations
- *(Level 2) Investment* – Advancement, Education, Growth
- *(Level 3) Relationship* – Emotional, Attachment, Comfort, History, Relationships
- *(Level 4) Allegiance* – Total Commitment to Purpose

At the *Material Level (Level 1),* we include all physical forms of compensation. The biggest problem with this level is it can be highly competitive, and there is very little you can do to make it unique. You either are willing to give it, or you are not… Staying at this level will only attract people who are looking for a raise, and you will only retain them as long as you are willing to pay them more than other people. Retirement benefits, medical benefits, legal benefits, etc… can almost always be matched, so they provide very little security as well.

At the *Investment Level (Level 2),* we begin to offer things that are a little tougher to match. Opportunities for advancement are not always available in an organization (or so they think… I like to default to the fact that you are always looking to grow). However, the education you can get at some organizations provides great opportunity for someone's long-term professional career, and just an opportunity for growth can attract people who want to be a part of it. The downside is this still relies heavily on physical compensation, which can be offered almost anywhere. While it may be a little more exclusive, it still does very little to promote loyalty either way.

At the *Relationship Level (Level 3)*, we finally offer things that are unique and hard to duplicate. Engaging with our team at a personal level, investing in their lives, and just simply showing compassion automatically provokes reciprocation. I have seen employees go without pay checks for weeks while a business was waiting on contract compensation, due to their commitment to the relationship with the company. Is it because they were just lucky enough to find people like that? Of course not! It was the investment in the relationship that compelled them to be patient, and to support the business even without a direct reason.

Finally, at the *Allegiance Level (Level 4)*, we have something entirely different: a relationship in which the individual shares the same values, goals, vision, and purpose as the organization. This relationship is one in which they not only represent, but also evangelize the business whenever they can… making fully available all of their resources, personally and professionally, to see the organization succeed. In turn, the organization makes a commitment towards the success of the individual by providing all the tools necessary to be successful.

One of my favorite examples of living this standard is a company called Zappos. They are so committed to discovering and filtering the best representation for their company that they make a commitment like nothing I have ever seen. Zappos' recruiting practices are legendary for offering new employees $1,000 to not take the job after their probationary period, as a demonstration that physical compensation will not be an employee's only reason for working there.[10]

Cultures like this do not happen overnight, and do not happen on accident. They are deliberate because the organization understands that a company can only achieve the greatest of itself if it is getting the greatest from its people. As mentioned previously in this book, the secret to these organizations is the creation of a "**L.O.V.E.**ing" environment. A "**L.O.V.E.**ing" environment is one that encourages, recognizes, and rewards those who represent specific principles relating to the business.

**L** – Loyalty
**O** – Ownership
**V** – Vibrancy
**E** – Exemplify

**Loyalty**
When most business owners speak of "Loyalty," generally the focus is placed on the loyalty of the individual to the company, and not necessarily the loyalty the company shows to the team. Can we be realistic? Unless you are an emerging company in an emerging market, entry level people will outgrow your opportunity at some point and move on. Is this because they are not loyal? Of course not!

A common fear among business owners is that investing in your employee's development is more or less investing in your future competition. While this may be a reality in some cases, you only hurt yourself and your client if you decide to not develop them out of fear. By not equipping them while they represent your company, you risk poor production, incompetence, and substandard communication skills with your clients. This can damage critical relationships, void future opportunities, and/or destroy your brand. The truth is, even if a person begins their growth inside your organization, and due to limited opportunity is forced to move on to somewhere else, the growth of people is imperative. So the question becomes, how committed are you to the experience of your client, even if it means the people you have developed have the potential to take that knowledge elsewhere? If you knew it was at the risk of potentially losing the opportunity with your clients for the life of your business, I am sure it would be pretty high.

By making the commitment with people early on that you are dedicated to their success, you also set precedence on what can be expected of them. "Giving prior notice" and "Leaving the place better than when you left" can now be recognized as the standard, rather than the exception. Loyalty to their success is also never fearing the consequences of educating them, knowing that the alternative is worse. Just as technicians are made, not born, so are leaders and people who interact with our clients. I had an owner the other day come to me with a concern that his managers were not communicating with their team appropriately. Rather than focusing on their misconduct I asked, "Well, what training have you made available to them that would improve their communication skills?" As most people would probably figure out, the answer was none. It is surprising how comfortable some businesses are not qualifying the people who represent them. I have been around companies that have asked people to manage projects with no formal PM training (like a simple PMP Certification). They invest next to nothing in communication skills for their sales people or their client services reps. Across the board, most companies almost never invest in helping their people improve personally, something that can have a positive effect on both their personal and professional life. All because they fear that once they train someone, they may never fully see the benefit.

Can that happen?

Of course it can… But how much are you losing in your business with unqualified people and an environment that does not support the improvement of others?

Loyalty is about compassion and caring. So how "Loyal" are you to the people who work for you? Below are some steps you can take to demonstrate it even more:

1.  Change your perception of what loyalty is: Asking for them to be loyal to the company, without your business committing to their growth and prosperity isn't balanced. Loyalty is a two–way street.

2. Set the standard in your first interaction, and be committed to their success, regardless if it is with you long term or not. Let them know you expect them to be committed to the success of your company, also.

3. Like everything else, great people are developed! Always be training and making them better.

4. Make sure your compassion extends beyond work, support them whenever you can, and try to give them skills that will transfer in to all parts of their lives.

**Ownership**

Another misunderstood dynamic in business is Ownership. When most people are introduced to the idea, they immediately think of people owning their mistakes or taking initiative. While these are some elements of Ownership, they do not fully represent its meaning. The bigger picture of Ownership is taking responsibility for what is produced in every way possible including its improvement, production, and delivery. In addition, I have always held the belief that all companies should also include some sort of reward to its employees if the company is growing significantly, whether it be in profit sharing or bonuses. To me, a base salary is just that: a base, and any opportunity you have that you can reward people for their Ownership is a practice that pays off indefinitely. Ownership also means getting insight, input, and suggestions from everyone who represents the company. Often times, when the owner or management makes decisions, they do so with limited or no input from the people actually performing the work. As a result, the adapted change can seem burdensome, and in some cases can make the job of the people involved even harder. Involving everyone in the suggestion phase of the improvement process pays off in BIG dividends... If someone's idea is used, they become an immediate champion in its implementation. The changes that happen have an extra value to the person and people around them, so even when the changes are a burden, they are more accepted. Finally (and most of all), some of the best ideas come from the people who are actually using the equipment, which means your opportunity for success can be dramatically increased. Another immediate benefit is in the production phase of Ownership. As most business owners know, traditionally the drive for quality and standards comes from the top down. Management at every level is bogged down by focusing on making sure their team is meeting minimum quality standards. As a result, this leaves very little time for management to explore new opportunities to improve and set up your company for future success. Ownership at the production level means that every person takes responsibility for the deliverable, regardless if it is their "job" or not. By reducing the need for top-down quality control standards, the owner and management can instead focus on innovation and opportunity. It also prevents a great amount of conflict, frustration, and anxiety when leadership interacts with the team, because the commitment to quality is the same. Finally, it creates a great amount of pride when delivering the final product to the client. Having pride increases quality, but also ingrains the question "How can I make this better?", which in itself, has immeasurable benefits. Imagine, for a moment, if your entire team was asking that question constantly... How successful would your company be today?

On a final note, one thing that I have seen that has provided fantastic value for businesses is specifically incentivizing the commitment to growth of their employees. Rather than focusing only on cost of living increases and annual reviews for increases in compensation, recognize the efforts of people who take the initiative to improve their skill level. People who constantly focus on improving have higher potential, and produce at a higher level. It also demonstrates your commitment to their ongoing success. Regardless if your people take it upon themselves to improve or not, bringing in training professionals, having an in-house training coordinator, or designating outside courses, the company as a whole should always have a commitment to improve. The more you are focused on delivering the tools necessary for Ownership of your employees, the more focused they will be on taking Ownership in everything they are doing.

**Vibrance**

I could really end this chapter by saying "ENTHUSIASM IS CONTAGIOUS" and dropping the microphone. If people have an environment similar to a Christian retreat to go to everyday, how much would they dread the trip? Not at all! There is just something to be said about energy! When you have it, things move fast, tempo goes up; it's almost like a well-oiled track with no friction at all, moving from one stage to the next. Without it… well, anyone who has been in an energy depressed environment knows what it is like! It is a constant battle to get anyone to do anything, even if it is simple and in their job description. Sometimes it is hard to just get yourself started, and you are dependent on caffeine or some other type of stimulant to keep you going. Community commitment is almost non-existent and a "watching out for number one" mentality is common place.

People want to be inspired…they want to be swooned, and they want to be LIT UP!!! They want to lose the hours, and not even realize where they have all gone. Our fear of judgment, here in the United States, has caused us to become complacent, content, and borrrrrrring… always searching for something that would get our heart pumping, and interests peaked (Facebook anyone?).

Be intentional in finding ways to get your team excited, and make that the standard of your business. Don't let "being cool" get in the way of your teams enjoyment, and promote some type of competition everywhere you can. I'm not talking about sales contests and overwhelming standards. I am talking about things that are fun and that promote working together and critical thinking. I'm not talking about cash bonuses and big vacations all the time. Get some functional toys or some treats and make it fun! I mean, come on… High fives are free. I had an old friend who passed away a few years ago that really understood this concept, and took it to an exceptional level. Several times during the year, he would take his team of fifty employees and their families on excursions, just for fun. One year, he brought them all to a local theme park for the day. Another time, he rented out a Go-Cart track and paid for the arcade for the ones too little to ride. With him, it was always about passion and people… and everyone who worked for him—or that he provided for—knew it. Do you think he had people leaving for five dollars more an hour? Never happened! I am sure it is possible to take this concept too far, but I have yet to see it, personally. Chances are, what you would consider to be "too far" would not be far enough.

**Exemplify**

Our final part of a **L.O.V.E.**ing environment is "Exemplifying the people who take action towards your vision and purpose."

Far too often, we only recognize those who are not doing the right thing, or the ones that are increasing sales. If you look at this standard objectively, what you are saying is that as long as your employees don't do anything wrong, and they make sales for the company, they are your preferred type of employee… If that was the case, I doubt you would have made it this far in the book.

As you are making changes in your business, recognize the people who are taking ownership of them. If there is a guy or gal who constantly makes suggestions and is really participating, make an example of them. Do you have someone who has fully embraced the "Client Provision" mindset we have talked about throughout this book? You should give that guy or gal a MEDAL!

People will only do what gets recognized and monitored, so be careful with the messages you are putting out there. Ask yourself, are you being clear in your expectations of your people? Quite often, there are things that we say in public, but other things we keep behind closed doors. We may say that providing for the customer is the most important thing, but is that standard also executed when no one is looking? We could go on at great length dissecting what is said vs. what is really happening, but most people can figure out when their leadership is contradicting their words with their actions. The truth of the matter is, if you are rewarding what is happening behind closed doors, then that is what you will see most.

One other point I would like to make here is that a true reward should be based on the needs of the person receiving it, not on the needs of the person giving it. In 1992, Gary Chapman published *The Five Love Languages: How to Express Heartfelt Commitment to Your Mate.11* In it, he goes on to explain that people express and receive love in five different ways: words of affirmation, quality time, receiving gifts, acts of service, or physical touch. He also goes on to explain that even though we all express and receive love in these ways, there are certain ones that resonate at a higher level for each individual person, and by acknowledging and fulfilling their specific preference, they appreciate the sentiment that much more. Over the years, his books have sold over eight million copies, and have been rewritten for specific genres like teens, couples, men, women, etc… Finally a couple years ago, they came out with *The 5 Languages of Appreciation in the Workplace: Empowering Organizations by Encouraging People.12* It is a FANTASTIC adaptation of his original work that translates well to the business world. With it, you can gain a greater understanding of how to demonstrate gratitude towards your team when they exemplify your business. One more resource I would like to share is how to make this concept scalable for the long term. Another great book I have used for clients is Bob Nelson's, 1997 edition of *1001 Ways to Energize Employees13*. Personally, I have purchased in my library two of his continuing titles, *The 1001 Rewards & Recognition Field book: The Complete Guide and 1001 Ways to Reward Employees*. My next purchase will more than likely be *1501 Ways to Reward Employees*, which just came out in 2013. By using these two guides in conjunction with each other, learning the love language of the individual and then delivering it in a unique way through the examples given in Bob Nelson's books you can create an environment that represents the core of our faith. Understanding people at their level and communicating with them in a way that speaks directly to their hearts will…

I really hope the idea of a "**L.O.V.E.**ing" environment provides you with some great ideas on how you can get more out of your people, and how your people can get more from your business. I do not disagree that "Hiring Slow and Firing Fast" is a necessary truth as a business owner; however, it is our job to ensure that we have given our employees the best environment—and the best opportunity—before we reach that decision. For years, I have seen businesses struggle with the reality that they have to make hard choices, because they worry that their inadequacies are the reason for the employee's failure. Get rid of the doubt!

Give them everything they need to succeed, and leave very little doubt in your mind that the employee owns their fate, and not the business, or you. It is not cruel or something to be ashamed of. It is about making an honest decision about what is best for your business and those you provide for. I find myself constantly preaching this, so please excuse me, but being a Christian business doesn't include forgoing profitability, or constantly becoming a charity case. It is about providing for those in need through our services at the best of our ability, and through our financial success, being able to contribute to others! It is our time now as Christian business owners to implement what we have learned through our faith, in every part of our lives.

Promoting a **L.O.V.E.** ing environment is only a part of that puzzle. It is not fool proof, or a guarantee of any sort. You may not be able to retain every person, or help everyone succeed. In many instances, potential employees have to make decisions based on their financial needs. However, if you ask most people what prompted their final decision, other factors usually came into play.

Ultimately, implementing some of these strategies will aid in your effort to be more attractive, while at the same time help you deliver an environment that is more positive and productive. Therefore, the business will gain the full potential of every employee, and those you provide for will be the biggest winners.

## Chapter 11

# THE CALL TO FULFILLING YOUR PURPOSE IN THE WORLD

I pray that this book has provided you and your business with what it needs to serve God's purpose for you at an even higher level. As I wrote it, there were countless times my team and I felt driven by Providence, and towards its completion we began to witness the affect that the concepts in the book have had, even with my own clients. With my team's commitment towards being Available, Able, and Aware personally, I wanted to deliver the resources so that you could do the same. Now the call is on you to spread your blessing to others and live the purpose you were created for.

First, out of respect for the commitment made to our potential clients, you have a divine responsibility to improve how you do business and how you provide for those who call on you. When given that opportunity, we as Christians have to ensure that we will do everything in our power to represent the faith appropriately. This means we need to stop "serving customers," and instead, "provide for our clients." This book was written as a guide to help jumpstart that commitment, and I would suggest reading through it repeatedly until you fully grasp its contents.

Second, I feel the need to encourage you and other Christian businesses to "Look Faith First" in all your transactions from now going forward. All this means is that before making any purchase or decision, give a fellow Christian an opportunity to compete for your business. You don't have to necessarily buy from them, but give them the chance. By doing so, you open up a world of possibilities for their prosperity, as well as the prosperity of our faith community. This encouragement doesn't have to stop with you, either. If you were to share this idea with all the people that you come in contact with in your day-to-day life, imagine the potential impact!

Finally, I encourage you to seek out spiritual guidance, mentoring, and coaching. The path that you are going on will have its share of obstacles and hazards and you must do all you can to ensure that you are prepared for the journey both mentally and spiritually. The truth is, one of the most common themes of the Old and New Testament is the potential "snares" and "temptations" that can come from the accumulation of great wealth. By taking on this journey, Christians become vulnerable to those temptations of the world, as well as to those who may not want the Christian community to be successful. I remember a few years ago, while providing comfort and counsel to a friend who was closing his business, the release of fear in his heart while in his final days. As we talked about the next chapter in his life, he came to his own realization that he could not be trusted with the wealth a successful business would have provided and that his service to God would be better in pastoral ministry. Now, it was a challenge for me to accept such a flesh-guided belief, personally, but I knew how he felt and have come across others who feel the same. This is why I truly believe that everyone needs a guide to help them through their journey…A spiritual beacon that will provide you with the direct anchor to the roots of faith and remind you that we are Stewards given our talents in trust…Someone that will provide you aid in fulfilling Gods purpose for you, both intentionally and purely. Having a guide is not really a luxury; it's a necessity with the world we work in today.

My brothers and sisters in Christ, again I wish you blessings on your journey. Please feel free to share your stories of success with us, so that we may share them with others. Your success will encourage and enable our fellow brothers and sisters to take part in changing how we as Christians represent business.

I hope my team and I were able to provide you with what you needed to get started down the path God has for you and your business. Enjoy the overwhelming fulfillment that comes from being a STEWARD of God's gift to you and all the blessings that come with it. While the changes for each business owner may be unique for their business, the next step for everyone is to TAKE ACTION! Re-engage your faith with your business, make providing for others the driving force of everything you do for optimal personal and business success.  Don't forget to go to www.GodsBusinessTheBook. com for additional resources to help you take action and succeed quickly.

As a final request, if you have felt drawn to our mission and know a Coach or Consultant that shares the same vision that we have illustrated here, you would bless us both by sending them to our site at www.lookfaithfirst.com, and having them submit their interest. Part of our calling is to fulfill every need in this journey for those who take it to task, and we would be eager to work with anyone who would champion it.

As always, may God continue to bless you and others around you!

Coach West

# ENDNOTES

1 Blanchard, Kenneth H. Raving Fans: A Revolutionary Approach to Customer Service. New York: Morrow, 1993. Print.

2 "German American Corner: STUDEBAKER BROTHERS." German American Corner: STUDEBAKER BROTHERS. Davitt Publications., 1996. Web. 12 Feb. 2015.

3 "The Value Proposition Canvas in 5 Minutes:." Business Model Generation. N.p., n.d. Web. 12 Feb. 2015.

4 "The Business Model Canvas in 2 Minutes:." Business Model Generation. N.p., n.d. Web. 12 Feb. 2015.

5 Michelli, Joseph A. The New Gold Standard: 5 Leadership Principles for Creating a Legendary

Customer Experience Courtesy of the Ritz-Carlton Hotel Company. New York: McGraw-Hill, 2008. Print.

6  "Timeline | The Deming Institute." Timeline | The Deming Institute. The W. Edwards Deming Institute, 2012. Web. 12 Feb. 2015.

7  Kroc, Ray, and Robert Anderson. Grinding It Out: The Making of McDonald's. Chicago: H. Regnery, 1977. Print.

8  CTIA—The Wireless Association. "Cell Phone Subscribers in the U.S., 1985–2010." Infoplease. Infoplease, 2007. Web. 12 Feb. 2015.

9  "Startup Business Failure Rate By Industry." Statistic Brain RSS. N.p., n.d. Web. 12 Feb. 2015.

10  Taylor, Bill. "Why Zappos Pays New Employees to Quit–And You Should Too." Harvard Business Review. Harvard Business School Publishing., 19 May 2008. Web. 12 Feb. 2015.

11  Chapman, Gary D. The Five Love Languages: How to Express Heartfelt Commitment to Your Mate. Chicago: Northfield Pub., 1995. Print.

12  Chapman, Gary D., and Paul E. White. The 5 Languages of Appreciation in the Workplace: Empowering Organizations by Encouraging People. Chicago: Northfield Pub., 2011. Print.

13  Nelson, Bob. 1001 Ways to Energize Employees. New York: Workman Pub., 1997. Print.

14. Kotler, Philip, and Waldemar Pfoertsch. B2B Brand Management. Berlin: Springer, 2006. Print.

## *Is Your Business Ready to Fulfill Its Purpose?!*

If so, Look Faith First is ready to provide you with the inspiration, resources, and direction you need to MAKE IT HAPPEN!

If your group or organization is ready for a more engaging and hands on relationship, we have put together group, individual, and team coaching packages that can fit into any budget and fulfill ANY PURPOSE, BIG OR SMALL!

In addition, if your group or organization will benefit directly from the Client Provision standard laid out in this book, or one of our other featured trainings/workshops that helps you to fulfill GOD'S PURPOSE FOR YOU, you can contact us directly at info@lookfaithfirst.com

Thank you, again, for supporting our calling, and remember to share *God's Business* with anyone who is ready to answer their call!

In appreciation for buying this copy of God's Business and supporting the Look Faith First movement, we have a special gift just for you! Along with the Fast Action Implementation Guide we have put together for you on www.GodsBusinesstheBook.com, we have enclosed a voucher on the next page that entitles you and your business to one complementary discovery session and one full coaching session, to aid you in your journey.

As always, may God continue to bless you and others around you!

God Bless,

Coach West

This voucher entitles you to

**_ONE_ DISCOVERY SESSION** and

**_ONE_ FULL COACHING SESSION**

for qualified businesses and organizations.

*You really can't imagine how*
*big the sky is until you fly,*
*you don't know how*
*big the ocean is until you sail,*
*and you don't know the true talents*
*you have been blessed with or what*
*you are capable of until*
*you partner with God and*
*set out to fulfill your Purpose!*

—Frederick "Coach" West III